Invisible Kingdom

Short Theological Engagements with Popular Music

Short Theological Engagements with Popular Music features theologians who have a passion for particular popular artists and who offer robust theological engagements with the work of that artist—engaging a song, an album, or a whole body of work over a career. Books in the series are accessible, yet deep both in their theological and musical engagement. Each book foregrounds ideas of interest in the musician's work, first, and puts these into conversation with the context and culture, second, and the Christian tradition, third. Each book, therefore, includes analysis of the cultural artifact, cultural context, and the relation to Christian tradition. Each book endeavors, as well, to speak with vitality to the challenges of living with God's mercy and justice in today's world.

Invisible Kingdom

The Waterboys, *Fisherman's Blues*, and the Re-enchantment of the World

Richard S. Briggs

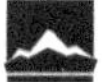 CASCADE *Books* • Eugene, Oregon

INVISIBLE KINGDOM
The Waterboys, *Fisherman's Blues*, and the Re-enchantment of the World

Short Theological Engagements with Popular Music

Cascade Books
An Imprint of Wipf and Stock Publishers
199 W. 8th Ave., Suite 3
Eugene, OR 97401

www.wipfandstock.com

PAPERBACK ISBN: 978-1-5326-0782-0
HARDCOVER ISBN: 978-1-5326-0784-4
EBOOK ISBN: 978-1-5326-0783-7

Cataloguing-in-Publication data:

Names: Briggs, Richard S., 1966–, author.

Title: Invisible kingdom : the waterboys, fisherman's blues, and the re-enchantment of the world / Richard S. Briggs.

Description: Eugene, OR : Cascade Books, 2024 | Series : Short Theological Engagements with Popular Music | **Includes bibliographical references and index.**

Identifiers: ISBN 978-1-5326-0782-0 (paperback) | ISBN 978-1-5326-0784-4 (hardcover) | ISBN 978-1-5326-0783-7 (ebook)

Subjects: LCSH: Scott, Mike, 1958–. | Waterboys (Musical group). | Popular music—United States—Religious aspects.

Classification: ML3921.8.R63 .B74 2024 (paperback) | ML3921.8.R63 .B74 (ebook)

VERSION NUMBER 10/03/24

To Josh, Kristin, and Matthew

For sharing a love of more kinds of music than I can fully appreciate and for filling the house with the music they made over many years

Theoretically we are all pagans in Arcadia. . . . Nevertheless, Christian theology is always breaking in.

—C. S. Lewis, *Oxford History of English Literature*, 342

Contents

Acknowledgments

This is a book I long wanted to write but was never really sure I would, until Chris Spinks nurtured it into existence over several years of friendly encouragements. His friendship and expert advice are much missed—sadly he died just as this book was going to press. For the everlasting record: heartfelt thanks to Chris for such wisdom and support. I am grateful also to Christian Scharen for welcoming the book into the series, and to all at Wipf and Stock who have helped to produce the finished volume.

My musical education largely skipped over technical matters. I play guitar with enthusiasm but little finesse. For reasons unknown I have then had the joy of seeing all three of our children develop a wide range of musical skills and know-how. They have reacted with some bemusement to the news that I was writing a book about the Waterboys, but have encouraged me with good humor, various bits of technical information, and recommendations of other things I might prefer listening to. Even so, and with great delight, I dedicate this book to all three of them. The musicological aspects of this analysis, such as they are, are the result of their efforts to educate me, especially Josh, who "read through" the *Fisherman's Blues* album with me, while Kristin and Matthew over many years answered multiple questions on musical matters popular and technical. I would still like to claim all the errors and unfashionable opinions as my own.

Three moments finally propelled the actual writing of this long-planned book. The first was involvement in the "U2 Studies" conference in Belfast in summer 2018.[1] There I met several people, including Steve Stockman, who regaled me with tales about the Waterboys' great Irish adventure. In the opening chapter here I mention two Irish friends who first put me in touch with the music of the Waterboys. With one I have lost contact (hi Rebecca!), but Olwyn Adams and her wonderful family have hosted us often in Dublin over the years, and enthused about life and good music always: to Olly, Dave and the family many thanks.

My wife Melody has accompanied me to see the Waterboys in concert several times, and is willing to go as far as saying "I like some of their music." *Room to Roam* is her favorite. I am as always indebted to her for love and support in all things, not least in looking after me during a period of recovering from major operations in the very same summer that the world got locked down by a virus. The result was an unexpected gift of time and peace in which to pick up this book once more—the second moment where I made some progress.

The third and final motivation was during a restful summer when we visited the west of Ireland, including a chance to visit Spiddal among other places. Suitably

1. My paper "Sarajevo and the PopMart Lemon" was published in the resulting essays, to the mystification of my theological college colleagues at the time.

inspired, I suddenly found the book came together quickly, in ways described in chapter 2 below.

In the spirit of *Fisherman's Blues* itself I conclude with the ultimate acknowledgment: Thank you, God, for life, love, and music.

A Note on Song Identification

As described properly in chapter 6, but already relevant before that, the Waterboys' *Fisherman's Blues*—the 1988 album—exists in multiple versions. The "definitive" one is a six CD box set, called *Fisherman's Box* (2013), for which Mike Scott, the chief creator of all the Waterboys' albums, helpfully compiles its 121-song running list in chronological order of recording. It is frequently useful, for my description of what is going on, to label a song or version by locating it on this 6CD-running order. To do this I abbreviate to *FBx* with the number of the disc followed by / the number of the song on that disc. So for example:

FBx 1/5 = disc 1, song 5: "Fisherman's Blues," the original "first song on the album" and its title track

As a pointer to how vast the *Fisherman's Blues* project became, here is a checklist of the six CDs, and when and where they were recorded:

FBx 1 = Dublin, January 23, 1986

FBx 2 = Dublin, March–September 1986

FBx 3 = Berkeley, December 2–7, 1986

FBx 4 = Dublin, December 1986—February 1987

FBx 5 = Dublin, March–May, 1987 (plus one remix in November 1987)

FBx 6 = Spiddal, County Galway, April–June 1988 (after songs 1–3 on a warm-up day in Dublin, late March 1988)

Scott's own view is that the sessions on discs 1–3, largely playing live in the studio, made good use of studio time in between various live and touring commitments, albeit without getting very close to a releasable album, while disc 6 represents finally bringing the project to completion in the West of Ireland. It is the six months captured on discs 4 and 5 that are the period where he got lost: "burned out" and "making suspect decisions." As he tells it, exaggerated and uninformed rumor "easily turns into 'They spent three years in a studio, man,' even if we didn't. The six Windmill [Lane studios, Dublin] months of '87 were quite enough, thank you very much."[1]

So when I simplify by saying "they spent three years on this," all of that is what I am referring to.

1. Scott, "Track by Track."

1

Meditation in the Fisherman's Tool-Shed

Three Portraits

The fiddler stands poised, on the roof of the world. His is the song that was sung before the world began. His is the voice of the resistance to empire: the fiddler on the roof of legend, from the first to the twentieth centuries and beyond, whether Rome was burning or imperial Russia was crumbling. He opens the eyes as he opens the ears, drawing down music through the long dark night of the modern age. For those with ears to hear, he is weaving the magical spell of the Waterboys' *Fisherman's Blues*. The long winter is over, and the world is waking up.

For this mystical, melancholy, majestic and mad journey: hold fast. See how the world was lost and where it got us. And see how the Waterboys wrestled it back again.

Three portraits . . .

***

A man is in the toolshed. He is an Oxford lecturer and lover of literature, a Cambridge Professor of Medieval and Renaissance Literature, a fantasy author and a writer of children's books. He is C. S. Lewis, and he is looking along a ray of light. Or at least, he is writing about looking along a ray of light, in his piercing exploration of what it is to know, and what we know.[1]

The spark of imagination mixed with the deep wells of reflection triggers a wondrous insight. He realizes that you can either look at the light, or look along it. Some traditions of the Western world have specialized in thinking that looking at the light is the mode of understanding: we become experts in the light, know all about it, and write learned books on various aspects of light theory. Meanwhile, a whole world goes about its wandering way in sore need of illumination, but never likely to read such books, increasingly—indeed—not even likely to benefit from such books third or fourth hand as they try to trickle down the rarefied paths of academia. Rather, it is by looking along the light that the seer can illuminate our paths. To look along the light is, in Lewis's terms, a "stepping inside."

We end up knowing *through* the light, looking at what it lights for us.

Maybe if C. S. Lewis had been a musician he would have let this idea work its way into music. His writing occasionally touched on music, which is not the same as writing about it, but he did try to show how song can create worlds. He showed Aslan singing a new world into being, for example. But he was not the one who could transform this blinding flash of insight into a soundtrack for re-enchantment. It was Lewis's calling to point the way: a way "further up and further in."[2]

1. See Lewis, "Meditation in a Toolshed."

2. Lewis, *Last Battle*, the phrase being the title of chapter 15.

***

A man is walking the bridges of Konigsberg. It is around 1780 and you can set your watch by him. He is a professor of philosophy, still working on that first big difficult book. He is Immanuel Kant. He is thinking about truth, beauty, and religion within the limits of reason alone.[3]

Herr Professor Kant is in fact attempting nothing less than the project of leading the human race by the hand out of the bounds of its self-imposed immaturity. Toward Enlightenment. Enlightenment (*Aufklärung*) he defines, with a sense of invincible progress out of the "dark" ages, as "the human being's emergence from his self-incurred immaturity.[4] . . . *Sapere aude!*[5] Have courage to make use of your own understanding! is thus the motto of enlightenment."[6] Perhaps if you listen carefully you can hear the sound of the Big Music warming up in the wings: songs to rule the world by; music with your fist in the air; the adrenaline rush of the stadium grand entrance . . .

Kant just taps his pipe and keeps walking. But it is a smoker's pipe, clouding the air and blurring the vision. Maybe if Kant had been a musician we would be living in a very different world, but he thought music a rather impermanent aesthetic mode of expression at best. Maybe if Kant had been a musician then the inner spirit and the

---

"Further Up, Further In" would become the name of a song on the Waterboys' *Room to Roam* album (1990).

3. Kant (1724–1804) published his *Critique of Pure Reason* in 1781—his first book when he was then in his late fifties. His subsequent *Religion within the Limits of Reason Alone* was published in 1793.

4. I adjust the translation here from "minority." *Unmündigkeit* is better (and more pointedly) "immaturity."

5. "Dare to be wise" (from Horace).

6. Kant, "What Is Enlightenment?," 17.

outer reality of the physical world would never have been so rent asunder. But alas, there was no music in his musing. So in his wake the curtain of silence descended gloomily over a thousand and one rain-drenched nights—not for the modern world the storied nights of Scheherazade. Music became a privatized hobby for one's leisure time, a down-time activity to be filed under "entertainment." The "real world" slouched toward brick and mortar, paperwork and administration.

Maybe Kant had the wrong sort of pipe.

***

A man walks into a bar and orders a Guinness. He has come to hang out in Dublin for a week with his friend the fiddler. But like all great creative weeks, this one will run and run, stretching in the end to six whole years.[7]

He will make his away slowly across all Ireland, coming to the dream at the end of the world. He will take hold of the Big Enlightenment project by the scruff of the neck, and wrestle it to the ground, like Jacob wrestling the angel, unwilling to let it go without a blessing. He will make music that lets loose life in all its fullness. Before the sun rises, he will have waylaid the juggernaut of the modern age and created one of the most remarkable albums of this or any other time. One that is at least three in fact, and probably many more. But he too will limp, bearing the scars of wrestling the spirit of our times. Of rending the veil that blinds us from the sea and sky, and which consigns us to the technocratic dream of order, control, and mastery.

Along the way he will invoke entire realms of muses and mythical beings, always waiting in the wings of heaven to play their parts. Unlike another famous veil rending, this

7. Scott, *Adventures*, 90.

one will work from the bottom to the top, laying hold of the descending darkness to strike up a tune that will lead from station on to station to the farthest outpost of the West, or at least the European West, at the last stop before America . . . Galway and the far shores of the West of Ireland. This space stretches out to the magical landscapes of Connemara, the Gaelic-speaking peninsula that runs West out of Galway City, along the north shore of Ireland's great Atlantic inlet, Galway Bay.

The man is Mike Scott, founder and leader of the Waterboys. And he is rowing out to the middle of the bay, far away from the dry land and its bitter memories. Behold: the still-motion capture of abandonment and love, in a perfectly-judged two-step dance. Nothing but the starry skies above.

Will we be loosened from chains that hold us fast? Will we receive, embrace even, the minority report—there is another way to live.

***

Welcome to the story of *Fisherman's Blues*, the album. Or at least to some of its many possible stories, stretching backwards and forwards in time. It is a story that takes place in the shadows of the changing of the guard of the Western world.

There is a train coming, and it looks like a gospel train, it sounds like a gospel train, and it feels like a gospel train, so is it . . . could it be . . . ? There is only one way to find out.

Get on board.

2

On My Way to Heaven

Where Are We Going?

I fell in love with the music of the Waterboys from the first moments of the first song of theirs I ever heard.

I was a young idealist spending 1990 on an international mission team in a French-speaking industrial city in Belgium, and there were two young Irish ladies on the team who knew more about rock and pop music than I did. Early summer we were commissioned to redecorate a local house that had fallen into disuse and disrepair. As we began stripping wallpaper one of my Irish colleagues put on a cassette, back in those technologically clunky days, and the swirling saxophone and startling pounding intro to "Don't Bang the Drum" filled the empty room. By the time its opening lyric arrived 1:56 in to the *This Is the Sea* album—"Well here we are in a special place. . . "—I was captivated. I still think it is one of the most powerful opening moments of any rock album. Who was this mystical, luminous high-octane band?

Later that summer our team was charged with another mundane task, washing up the cups and plates from a huge church social event we had hosted. It was the turn of my other Irish colleague to provide a cassette, cued up—it so happened—to side two of another album, *Fisherman's Blues*, and thus opening with the gentle Celtic strum of "And a Bang on the Ear." Instead of being ushered into the sacred space of "Don't Bang the Drum," this song opened out easily on to a friendly barn-dance of a wistful lyric of lost love laid over what sounded like a local ceilidh band. Who now was this relaxed, joyful group of low-key fiddlers and tin-whistlers?

The answer to both those questions is the same, as anyone interested to read this book doubtless realizes. This double introduction to the Waterboys proved unforgettable. Furthermore, the mystery of how their third album (1985's epic *This Is the Sea*) was related to their fourth album (1988's elegiac *Fisherman's Blues*) immediately intrigued me. In the thirty-some years since that summer, I have continued to listen to and to love the music of the Waterboys. I have learned a good deal of the answer to that question of what happened between 1985 and 1988, not least via Mike Scott's autobiography, which is one of the most engaging rock music autobiographies ever written.[1] I have also reflected at length on what exactly constitutes the extraordinary experience of *Fisherman's Blues*, in its forms both as a single 1988 album and then—unfolding gradually over twenty-five more years of releases—as the full musical record of the three years that went into making it.

This book essays an argument that the genius of this album, and its associated later expansions, lies in immersing the listener in a spiritual and transcendent reality: part infused by the joining of rock music to more traditional forms of Irish music and part opened up by reveling in a receptivity to the light and life that comes from beyond our daily world. In the process the music transforms our

1. Scott, *Adventures*.

world—what I will call a "re-enchantment" of our reality. The album is also fun, which I will try not to let slip away between the cracks of accounting and analysis.

In an early draft I tried to marshal all this reflection into a tight logical argument that moved historically and analytically through the story of the Waterboys, the story of *Fisherman's Blues*, and the conceptuality of re-enchantment. The results lacked . . . enchantment. Driving through Connemara myself one day, and breathing in the Irish air (/culture/spirit/ . . .) I realized that the way this book needed to work was more like the way the track-listing for *Fisherman's Blues*, or even more its follow-up *Room to Roam*, worked. In other words: creatively juxtaposed fragments of argument, celebration, reportage, and theological construction. Hence the dozen or so chapters of this book, in a loose logical progression, but relaxed enough to enjoy the diversions along the way.

Two things this book is not, then, in order to avoid some false expectations. First it is not a detailed historical account of who did what and how *Fisherman's Blues* happened. A brief version of this story is told as and when it becomes relevant (mainly in chapters 3, 6, and 9 below). But I am less interested in what lies behind the music, and more interested in what opens up in the world in front of the music; the world into which the music invites us. As a lyricist operating in various poetic registers, Mike Scott himself might agree that what he thinks any one of his songs is about is not the only interesting account of what the song is saying. I try to be attentive to the rich and resonant layers of musical and lyrical intrigue that constitute *Fisherman's Blues*. But other listeners would hear other things, inevitably and rightly so.

Secondly, in engaging in a theological account of the world as seen through the lens of *Fisherman's Blues*, I am not trying to co-opt Scott's personal aims or intentions to Christian themes and ideas, or to claim that the music is Christian in itself. Scott has been as clear as he can reasonably be on this point. Despite periods where he appeared and performed on Christian TV shows or was interviewed in Christian media, he saw no real link between what he was doing and Christian faith.[2] It is spirituality that interests him, and religion is only of help in so far as it offers a framing context for looking at spiritual questions. For example, his 1993–94 stay at Findhorn, a spiritual community in Scotland focused on matters of inner transformation and sustainable living, is a good example of his "religious" but not Christian spiritual engagement. It gave rise to 2003's *Universal Hall* Waterboys album, with songs such as "The Christ in You" that are not, in general, imbued with Christian sensibility.[3]

Perhaps he is drawn to gospel music in the same way as he is drawn to a wide range of musical forms: because when it works well it facilitates that quest for what lies beyond, or underneath, the more familiar styles and tropes of contemporary pop music.[4] I am very happy to respect that. I am not trying to pretend that what Scott is doing is other than it is.

At the same time, my own interests do lie in the direction of Christian theology, and this book is a contribution to a series of theological engagements with popular music. As will become clear, I find *Fisherman's Blues* invites a good deal of theological reflection on the nature of our life experience between the sea and the sky, which is—as I would

2. See Abrahams, *Strange Boat*, 174–76 and, e.g., the entertaining anecdote about appearing on Christian TV programmes with his "heretical, gnostic songs" in Scott, *Adventures*, 255.

3. See Scott, *Adventures*, 233–49.

4. Scott, "Fisherman's Blues," is particularly clear on this.

say—in all of God's good creation. So there is a certain amount of creative tension here between Scott's purposes and my own interests in what he has done. I am interested in the theological world opened up by the Waterboys, rather as Alan Jacobs, in his wonderful essay on "Thomas Pynchon as America's Theologian," is doing theological thinking in light of the theologically rich texts he is reading, even while those texts themselves are not apparently declaring a Christian theology.[5] I think I am trying to do for a rock album, and band, what Jacobs is doing for a novelist, and his work.

As long as one is clear about the difference between what the music opens up and what the musician(s) intended then there is no reason for this to be confusing. While writing I came across a relevant quote from Brian Eno, whose musical world is possibly even more wide-ranging and eclectic than that of the Waterboys. However, he was pausing to reflect over the fact that *The Dynamic Reverend Maceo Woods and the Christian Tabernacle Choir in Concert* is one of his favorite albums:

> I was worried about it at first. Why am I so moved by a music based on something that I just don't believe in? What I started to think was that one of the things we humans like doing is surrendering. We love to be in a situation where we're out of control, . . . you have to have another strategy and that involves some kind of surrender. Partly having faith in the other people who are with you, but also having faith in everything. The basic message of gospel is "everything's gonna be alright," and that's a fantastic message. A message of optimism. All of these songs, if

5. Jacobs, "Far Invisible." For full disclosure, I also discovered the C. S. Lewis epigram used in the present book via Jacobs, "Chronicles," 273.

> you listen to them, even the ones that are quite gloomy, they're really saying "it's gonna be alright." You'll get through it. That's the message I want to hear.[6]

There will be opportunity in what follows to probe a little more deeply some of the mismatch between gospel hope and the music of the Waterboys, or indeed to see how "everything's gonna be alright" is only one dimension of "the basic message of gospel," though certainly a real one. But for now all I want to say is that there are areas where *Fisherman's Blues* and gospel reorientation overlap.

One result is that this book heads off in a direction in which Scott himself likely has little interest. But again, it is not a matter of offering the one true account of what *Fisherman's Blues* is about. We are in pursuit of what *Fisherman's Blues* helps us to see elsewhere, to look along the light rather than at the light, in the terms of C. S. Lewis's meditative suggestion.

What is that we see when do this? To anticipate: we see a life re-enchanted with possibility, a life that I cannot but relate to the world as God's theater. The credits for the album, in all its forms, conclude with "Thank you God for life, love and music." Different listeners would fill out the significance of this affirmation differently. I take it in the direction of a theology of re-enchantment that opens windows on to and into God's own kingdom.

Such an argument about the theological possibilities in store here will be unfolded in what follows. Before we get to it, we turn to a brief history of the Waterboys (chapter 3), and then divert into a look at some fascinating parallels with a particular period in the career of Bob Dylan (chapter 4). It is from this link that I draw my title, *Invisible Kingdom*, for reasons explained there, and then expounded in

6. Eno, "Free, Open Spaces."

terms of disenchantment and re-enchantment in chapter 5. At various points I wondered if it was just *Fisherman's Blues* that I was interested in or the whole of the Waterboys' recorded output, which has continued to grow a-pace as I have made my leisurely way through writing this book. Chapter 6 fudges the issue by engaging briefly with their other recordings, though in a way that focuses around the achievement of *Fisherman's Blues*.

With the album now fixed in our sights, I lay out in chapters 7 and 8 two key reflections on what I think is going on, drawing on Tolkien's extraordinary piece "On Fairy-Stories" and on the various ways this weaves in and out of the Christian story, which is a topic that excited no small discussion between Tolkien and Lewis. Lewis's imprint is all over the Waterboys' Irish recordings, more for his grasp of mythological story telling and its power than his unique form of Christian narrative bricolage. But his relaxed blurring of the lines between Christian and fantasy literature suits my own purposes rather well. Now with opened eyes, or at least so I hope, we arrive at last in chapter 9 at a detailed "reading" (or should that be "hearing"?) of *Fisherman's Blues* itself.

If there is merit in seeing the world through this *Fisherman's Blues* lens, then where does it leave Christian faith in the world that the Waterboys are challenging—the world of the big music and the grand gesture and the pretensions to mastery? Chapter 10 offers a music-themed essay on a version of this question that perennially haunts me: "Is it possible to be a Christian in the West?" No surprise that the answer will be a strange mixture of "yes" and "no." We may all be pagans in the Western world, in the terms explored in this book, but Christian theology does keep breaking in . . .

I conclude with a final reflection on this musical odyssey, taking up some of the low-key humility of the song

"Strange Boat," in which Mike Scott seems to sing of his own journey even as it is still in process. The boat in question is "carrying the strangest crew that ever sinned." If we find ourselves in that self-description then perhaps after all we have hope?

Readers might find various ways through this map of the chapters to come. Read about the Waterboys particularly in chapters 3, 6 and 9. Reflect on the work of the inklings (Tolkien, Lewis, . . .) via chapters 5, 7, and 8. Join with the philosophers and critics in chapters 5 and 10. Or just pick a path at random, keeping an eye out along the way for Bob Dylan, for the Spice Girls, for fantasy novels old and new . . . .

Do all roads lead to the West of Ireland?

3

Headlong into the Heartland

A Brief History of the Waterboys

Fisherman's Blues is the fourth Waterboys album, released in October 1988, some three years after its predecessor, *This Is the Sea*. Eschewing the "big music" sound of the band's earlier albums, it incorporates traditional Irish music, folk, blues, and even occasional country stylings, to provide a very different feel from anything the Waterboys had done before.

Or at least that is how it looked to the slightly bemused music press, casual fans, and popular media of the day. Clearly something strange had happened along the way. In this chapter I try to tell enough of the story of the Waterboys to explain what it was.

Born in 1958 in Edinburgh, Mike Scott formed the Waterboys in 1983. He took the name from an obscure line in Lou Reed's harrowing song "The Kids" from Reed's 1973 *Berlin* album: "I am the Water Boy . . . ."[1] Reed's *Berlin* is probably one of the darkest albums ever made, but the way he tells it Scott borrowed the name without any real

1. Abrahams, *Strange Boat*, 44.

reference to its original context. He just thought it sounded good. Over time Charles Kingsley's 1863 novel *The Water Babies: A Fairy Tale for a Land Baby* would seem a more auspicious reference point, but it was not Scott's source.

Scott had had brief spells recording solo and leading a band called Another Pretty Face, which included Anthony Thistlethwaite on saxophone. His earliest solo recording sessions grew into the work that produced the first two Waterboys' albums: their self-titled debut in 1983, and *A Pagan Place* in 1984. The core of the band included Thistlethwaite, Kevin Wilkinson on drums, occasionally Roddy Lorimer on trumpet, and in due course and up until 1985 Karl Wallinger on keyboards.

Even from early days there could be a disconnect between the membership of the live performing band and the group of people assembled together in the studio for recording sessions. In truth, any attempt to track membership of the group is doomed to never-ending complexity. It is often and probably rightly said that among rock musicians the Waterboys have had more members than any other group—well over eighty by all counts including all those listed on the band's official website—and there is no need to try to mention them all here. Two further members who would become important during the time of *Fisherman's Blues* were Trevor Hutchinson, on bass, and most prominently the Irish fiddler Steve Wickham. Wickham was previously better known outside Ireland for playing violin on a couple of the songs on U2's *War* album in 1983, including their startling (non-)protest song "Sunday Bloody Sunday." It was Wickham whom Scott visited in early 1986 for the week that stretched to six years, the week that kick-started much of *Fisherman's Blues* no less. Although he departed from the Waterboys in 1990, leading in the end to a hiatus in the group's official existence, he rejoined around 2000 and remained the one semi-permanent fixture of the band alongside Scott for some twenty more years or so.

In the early years the Waterboys were London-based, and seemed to have their sights set squarely on dominating the world of mainstream rock music. In the UK in the early 1980s, caught in a kind of post-punk/post-new-wave moment, this was a somewhat portentous place to be. Many bands were given to displays of exaggerated earnestness in interviews. The early Waterboys seemed to vie for the same sort of public space as was inhabited by Scotland's Simple Minds or Big Country, or early U2 as typified by their *War* album. Be that as it may, domination of this particular world looked increasingly like a target within the Waterboys' grasp as they progressed.

The early sound of the group was dubbed "the big music," after the title of a (gloriously expansive) song from their second album. As such a label suggests, the style was loud, visionary, uplifting. It aspired to be stadium-filling. It also points to a certain striking self-confidence in presentation and performance, which is very much characteristic of the early Waterboys. This phase of their career peaked with their third album, 1985's *This Is the Sea*, notable for its inclusion of their best known song, the wondrous and anthemic "The Whole of the Moon." It could have—should have—been a huge hit, and indeed eventually went to no. 3 in the UK charts upon reissue in 1991, when it also won an Ivor Novello award. But with the world seemingly at their fingertips, Scott's uneasy relationship with fame began to step up a gear. He was cautious about committing to TV performances, to interviews, and to the whole rigmarole of self-publicity that seemed to go with being a rock star. In 1985 "The Whole of the Moon" crept into the top 30, largely under-publicized, and faded from view.

Attempts to produce a follow-up album to *This Is the Sea* got waylaid as Scott moved to Dublin, recruiting Steve Wickham into the increasingly fluid line-up. He began to explore not just a wide range of blues, gospel, and folk styles but increasingly the deep riches of more traditional Irish music and its accompanying spirituality. This was unexpected territory for any rock band. Although the Waterboys had never been an Irish band, they effectively began to function as one as time wore on. In the words of *World Music: The Rough Guide*, "Some cynics claim that Scotsman Mike Scott decided to give Irish music back to the Irish when he set up camp in Spiddal, County Galway in the late 1980s, but his impact can't be underestimated."[2] Eventually, after recording well over one hundred songs in two and a half years of on-off sessions and finally settling in for a seven week stint in Spiddal in County Galway on Ireland's west coast to try to finish the album, Scott pulled together a single-disc fifty-two-minute version of *Fisherman's Blues*—a brief and inadequate testament to the odyssey of all that had happened.

Even as originally released, the album is a fascinating and mystical celebration of life and love. It was hardly what anyone would have expected of the Waterboys up to and including 1985. Sure enough, it was not the making of them commercially either. To an increasingly bemused listening world, they followed it in 1990 with *Room to Roam*, which was nestled even more securely in traditional forms of Irish music. It included an energetic cover version of the folk standard "The Raggle-Taggle Gypsy" that gave a name to this period of the Waterboys' history: the raggle-taggle band. But then just as suddenly, the line-up changed (in particular Steve Wickham left) and Scott took a stream-lined

2. O'Connor, "Ireland," 188. The brief entry on the Waterboys concludes, cuttingly, with "He's since moved on, found God, and moved on again."

rock band back out for live concerts in 1990. By the time of the sixth album, 1993's *Dream Harder*, recorded in New York, the Waterboys was essentially Mike Scott solo again, plus whichever session musicians he wished to bring in.

Through the rest of the 1990s Scott released records in his own name, but increasingly the distinction between "Waterboys" and "Mike Scott" ceased to be useful. Eventually Scott would say their music was all one and the same: "To me there's no difference between Mike Scott and The Waterboys; they both mean the same thing."[3] Thus the "re-forming" of the Waterboys with 2000's *A Rock in the Weary Land* was more of a change of emphasis than a radical switch. Here the tone was harder. Scott was back in the rock and roll heartland, although older and seeming somewhat more cynical than when he had last inhabited it.

Subsequent Waterboys albums have ranged over quite the sonic landscape, from pop to quieter and more reflective material, back to harder rock. It is all of a piece with Scott's career that one finds the increasingly celebratory and eclectic use of a truly wide range of styles and tones even on one release. In many ways this is most clearly showcased on 2017's sprawling but engaging double-CD *Out of All This Blue*. As of the time of writing, the Waterboys continue to tour, to record, and to enjoy and explore life with an infectious enthusiasm.

The most note-worthy twenty-first-century Waterboys' album, at least with regard to my focus in this book, is the splendid project of setting W. B. Yeats's poetry to music on 2011's *An Appointment with Mr. Yeats*. Here the close fit

3. This quote is well attested, and is used for example on the back cover of Abrahams, *Strange Boat*. A note on Wikipedia said, "Scott has stated on numerous occasions that he sees no qualitative or creative difference between the music produced under the two brand names" (Wikipedia, s.v. "The Waterboys Discography," https://en.wikipedia.org/wiki/The_Waterboys_discography).

of Scott's lyrically expansive musical vision and love of Irish culture is thrown into sharp relief by way of the great Irishman Yeats's poetry. It was a marriage of voices first fully attempted as the closing track to *Fisherman's Blues* back in 1988, on "The Stolen Child." Both then and in 2011 the results are fascinating and captivating.

This outline story of the Waterboys will serve for our purposes. It can be easily researched in further detail, in these information-overloaded days. Anyone can look them up online and read either their own official web-site[4] or the standard resource of our age, Wikipedia.[5] In fact the Wikipedia page of the Waterboys offers a little case-study in how to assess online information, due to an interesting experience once recounted by Mike Scott himself in Britain's *Guardian* newspaper.

Failing to resist the ever-present temptation to search for his own name on the internet, Scott came across the Waterboys' Wikipedia page and read through it. Overall he was pleasantly impressed by both its accuracy and its thoughtfulness. Inevitably, there were many and various small points that grated, and some of which were simply wrong as a matter of historical record, as he himself was uniquely well-placed to see. He edited them anonymously. Lo and behold, all his edits were promptly undone, and in due course he was contacted (still as an anonymous source) to be told that he needed to cite evidence to make the changes he had proposed. The irony, and indeed the tale itself, is worthy of a short story by Jorge Luis Borges.

4. mikescottwaterboys.com. A fan-run web-site that also contains a large amount of relevant and well-documented information is waterboys.org.uk.

5. Wikipedia, s.v. "The Waterboys," https://en.wikipedia.org/wiki/The_Waterboys.

However, on this occasion there was a happy ending. Scott wrote about this experience elsewhere, and news of this got back to the page editors of the Wikipedia account, with the result that they were able to communicate and come to an agreement. Scott himself wrote "my conscience said gently: is the subject of an entry the best and most objective person to unconditionally correct it?"[6] And yet . . . a subject aware of these issues and also in command of the history is certainly a key resource of some kind. All this to say that in fact the Wikipedia entry on the Waterboys is actually a very good account, as Scott acknowledged in his write-up of the incident.

In addition, there is a treasure-trove of a biography of Scott and the band written by Ian Abrahams in 2007, and then in 2012 Scott's own autobiographical account, *Adventures of a Waterboy*. In their completely different ways—the one external, enthusiastic, measured, and occasionally critical; the other internal and startlingly illuminating about the creative whirlwind of being at the heart of the Waterboys' life—these two books fill out the basic account admirably. There is indeed no shortage of information.

Here I take my leave from any attempt to pretend that I am offering a biography, or a history, of the Waterboys. Although I hope I will represent that history fairly, my focus is rather on critical and ultimately theological reflection on the recorded work produced.

But first, a word about Bob Dylan.

6. Scott, "Day I Downloaded Myself."

4

Invisible Kingdom (1)

The Dylan Connection

In terms of process, what ended up happening with *Fisherman's Blues* had happened before: hours and hours of music-making that eventually drifted far from being recorded for the purpose of commercial release. A disconnect enters in, and the music is freed up to explore its own vision regardless of what could be done with it commercially. In the end, its creators even begin to wonder whether it can be released.

When had it happened before? In 1967, with Bob Dylan's *Basement Tapes*.

The briefest version of this story is that following Dylan's extraordinary *Blonde on Blonde*, rock's first double-album, he had a motorcycle accident in upstate New York, retreated to a haven far away from the prying eyes of the media, and hung out with friends in a band that was to become known, eventually, as "The Band." Tape rolling, they passed the time at a house in West Saugerties in upstate New York, in fact in its basement, recording what became known as "the basement tapes." It was not, at the time, released.

Blonde on Blonde was rock's first double-album—released in May 1966 when Dylan was at the center of Beatle-esque levels of press and fan attention. The format was so new that no one, Dylan included, could really fathom how it worked. Side four had one song on it ("Sad-Eyed Lady of the Lowlands") which did run for over eleven minutes, granted, but so had "Desolation Row" at the end of his preceding (1965) album *Highway 61 Revisited*. If one compares the two albums *Blonde on Blonde* runs for effectively three album "sides," not four. But there it was: the invention of the double album.

Then likewise, the results of Dylan's recording sessions in New York state found their way on to rock's first (so-called) "bootleg" album, *Great White Wonder*. This vinyl double album, bearing a title but no artist's name, appeared mysteriously, illegally, and outside any system of official commercial release. This was July 1969, when Dylan was basically no longer appearing in public, and apparently not releasing new music.

Dylan resumed recording in 1969–70 with some low-key albums, resumed touring (with The Band, in fact) in January 1974, and returned to stunning musical form with *Blood on the Tracks* in January 1975. He then finally returned to the unreleased 1967 tapes, newly added to by a handful of more recent recordings apparently by The Band alone, to produce the official release of *The Basement Tapes* in June 1975. It was much loved, a big hit, and sold well, despite Dylan's bemused reflection that he thought everyone already owned it, via the illegal bootleg version(s).

The Basement Tapes is a delightful and undisciplined celebration of traditional, off-the-wall, and folk/blues orientated songs. It ends up rolling around in the relaxed reflections of American roots music, from children's rhymes to gospel-tinged celebrations, and from joy to lament, and stopping at many stations in between. The sense of release that came from just letting the tapes roll and not worrying about what ended up being recorded seems to have resulted in a glorious freedom to ignore all boundaries of what "should" be done and enjoy the creativity of the moment. It is, I sometimes think, the most fun to be had anywhere in listening to a rock star decide to ignore being a rock star.[1]

When Mike Scott started to draw down from some of the unreleased *Fisherman's Blues* recordings into a string of further releases, it became clear that in some ways the Waterboys' Irish sessions had themselves devolved into a *Basement Tapes*-style project. The creative joy of recording without a thought (or, possibly, without a focused thought) to commercial releasability . . . just as with Dylan it seems to have unleashed some of the most relaxed and celebratory music imaginable.

As a matter of fact, several Dylan songs made it on to the full *Fisherman's Blues* box set (*Fisherman's Box*), when it was finally released in 2013. They are:

- "Girl of the North Country" (*FBx* 1/2)—the classic traditional ballad from Dylan's second (and breakthrough) album, *The Freewheelin' Bob Dylan*, where it followed the opening and era-defining "Blowin' in the Wind."
- "I'll Be Your Baby Tonight" (*FBx* 1/7)—the gentle country-tinged ballad that closes Dylan's sparse official follow up to *Blonde on Blonde*, 1968's *John Wesley Harding*.
- "When the Ship Comes In" (*FBx* 2/5)—a fragment of Dylan's song from 1964's *The Times They Are A-Changin'*.

1. A good account of the whole adventure is Griffin, *Million Dollar Bash*.

- "Nobody 'Cept You" (*FBx* 4/12)—a wonderful full-on version of a song recorded by Dylan in 1973, and which finally surfaced on volume 2 of his (official) *Bootleg Series* in 1991. Dylan's version always feels slightly shambolic, at least at the beginning, whereas the Waterboys give it everything.
- "Buckets of Rain" (*FBx* 6/26)—the very last song of the whole *Fisherman's Blues* project, recorded near dawn on June 2, 1988, and (symbolically) the closing song of Dylan's *Blood on the Tracks* from 1975, when the work has been done and the fight is over.[2]

Now admittedly, it is hard for anyone to spend long celebrating rock's great mythology without getting buried deep in Bob Dylan's work or influence in one way or another. But this seems more than just a nod to Minnesota's finest, all things considered. I think it is evidence, appropriately piecemeal and low-key, that Mike Scott was enjoying acknowledging his love of Dylan's music in much the way that the whole *Fisherman's Blues* set of extended sessions was slowly evolving into a version of Dylan's own journey. It is not that the Waterboys were echoing Dylan, so much as that they were finding their way to the same territory that Dylan had earlier occupied.

More interesting than the formal similarities between the projects, then, is the strange way in which both Dylan and the Waterboys use these exercises in extended exploration of their (very different) roots to open up access to ways of thinking, seeing, and being that are so easily lost amidst

2. And note that "Drunken Head of Rimbaud Blues" (*FBx* 1/13) is deemed by Scott to be non-includable in the finished *Fisherman's Blues* album mainly because it lifts a line from Dylan's "Lily, Rosemary, and the Jack of Hearts," one of *Blood on the Tracks*' most unusual songs.

our modern preoccupations. We are looking at similar maps to similar (though by no means identical) territories.

Greil Marcus wrote that the results of Dylan's 1967 recordings opened up an *Invisible Republic*, his short-hand code for a world of almost lost traditional American self-expression, the "old, weird America."[3] Signaling goodbye to the world of rock and roll that Dylan had all but been controlling up until 1966, here he lets loose on reconnecting with something more primal. Thirty years after the *Basement Tapes* sessions Marcus writes of how Dylan and The Band caught hold of a confluence of American influences at a particular time and place:

> What they took out of the air were ghosts—and it's an obvious thing to say. For thirty years people have listened to the basement tapes as palavers with a community of ghosts—or even, in certain moments, as the palavers of a community of ghosts. Their presence is undeniable; to most it is also an abstraction, at best a vague tourism of specters from a foreign country.[4]

He goes on, turning the page, to the opening sentence of the next chapter: "As it happens, these ghosts were not abstractions." There were real people being rediscovered by way of Dylan's letting the tapes roll. The rest of Marcus's book is given over to celebrating the resulting "invisible republic," in and through the album—*The Basement Tapes* itself—that gives it voice.

When I came across Marcus's account I realized that I saw something comparable at work in *Fisherman's Blues*. Mike Scott is also accessing some of the same lost American voices, not least in the Hank Williams laments

3. Marcus, *Invisible Republic*. "The Old, Weird America" is the title of his fourth chapter.

4. Marcus, *Invisible Republic*, 86.

recorded early in the sessions ("I'm So Lonesome I Could Cry," "Lost Highway") and in self-penned material echoing the same world ("Lonesome and a Long Way from Home"). But in casting the net wider and deeper, Scott finds a different place from the republic of the "old, weird America." He finds his way instead to an invisible kingdom, indelibly marked by the traces of a once and future king. The question of who shall be king is an important one, and we shall come to it in good time. But what most interests me for the moment is the sense of looking for and indeed finding something like an overspill of grace in the world around us. This too is contact with reality, albeit not a physical one.

To put it another way, *Fisherman's Blues* is haunted by presence. But it is not just haunted by, but rather is full of, something else: Spirit. Scott had serenaded "Spirit" in a song of that name on *This Is the Sea*—only a fragment had made it on to the finished album but a longer version exists on the accompanying second disc of the re-released album in 2004. "Spirit" functions like a personal spiritual being in the way Scott imagines it. As he pulls back across Ireland on the way to making *Fisherman's Blues*, I think it is this sense of "Spirit" that gradually comes into view. Far enough away from the din of the modern world, nestled on the Galway peninsula, the Waterboys take us into the invisible kingdom, a kingdom luminous with God's spirit.

It is all about having eyes to see and ears to hear, and being able to grasp hold of the fullness of the creator in the midst of the creation. Or failing that, to recognize that the world around is indeed a creation of some kind at all. The full version of the album includes joyous and stunning versions of gospel standards such as "On My Way to Heaven" and "Meet Me at the Station," in both cases actually lyrically expanded in intriguing ways by Scott himself. There is gospel noise a plenty to explore. But I will argue that in fact the gospel—the good news—overflows the boundaries of the explicit gospel songs, and floods out into much of the work as a whole, baptizing the imagination with newly opened eyes of the heart. The phrase "eyes of the heart" I borrow from the New Testament (Paul's letter to the Ephesians—Eph 1:18). Alison Searle suggests that this is the way that the New Testament talks about the imagination: the ability to see, to really see the truth of things, by grasping the relationships of part and whole, or of experience-at-hand and overall context.[5]

We are up against the borders of (re-)enchantment. Time to call our next set of witnesses: Max Weber, with J. R. R. Tolkien lined up in the wings, and one of the twenty-first-century's most remarkable novels, Susanna Clarke's *Jonathan Strange and Mr. Norrell.*

5. Searle, *"Eyes of Your Heart,"* 32–40.

5

The River and the Sea

Disenchantment and Re-enchantment

Drawing 1985's *This Is the Sea* to a close, Scott had sung a series of once/now contrasts aiming at the conflict between what once had "tethered" the soul, and what now beckoned it on to fullness and freedom. "That was the river / this is the sea," ran the refrain. The song drew together much of the album's sense of longing. It espied a bigger, better, more liberating place. The only problem, it seemed, was that he could scarcely find words to describe it. It was "the sea." Yes, but what did that mean?

It is an evocative image, and serves its purpose well as the curtain falling at the end of the record. What is now interesting is to realize that Scott was on his way to finding out what sort of experience "the sea" might represent—an experience of enchantment, or perhaps re-enchantment, with the world.

A traditional perspective—a pre-modern one, let us note—was that the world was the theater of God's goodness. John Calvin says something like this in his mid-sixteenth-century commentary on the Psalms, and in various forms this idea persists into today's world. It was notably celebrated along the way by the Jesuit priest and poet Gerard Manley Hopkins (1844–89) whose 1877 poem "God's Grandeur" famously averred that the world is "charged with the grandeur of God," as it celebrates the claim that "nature is never spent." Hopkins lived out the final five years of his life in Dublin, in fact, rather unhappy as a university professor of the classics. His own experience of Ireland did not seem to bear out his most famous line.

By the late nineteenth century, of course, industrialization was taking its toll on the joys and enjoyment of nature. So it was into a world well primed to lament the loss of a sense of nature as God's creation, let alone a world wounded by war on an unprecedented industrial scale, that German sociologist and social scientist Max Weber (1864–1920) delivered a lecture at Munich University in 1917. In fact two lectures: "Science as a Vocation," and "Politics as a Vocation," seeking to see ways ahead from the crushing of the human spirit that was manifest not just in the war effort but in the technological ways of thinking that underlay vast swathes of modern life. In Weber's terms: "The fate of our times is characterized by rationalization and intellectualization, and, above all, by the 'disenchantment of the world.' Precisely the ultimate and most sublime values have retreated from public life."[1] Weber was talking about a contraction or eclipse of truth in modernity—the "magic" is gone and our hearts are left restless. In the uncomfortable words of a sympathetic recent commentator: "We all rush madly about—all the more madly as modern systems of transportation enable us to get almost anywhere—but we cannot say where we are going. Everybody is busy; nobody knows what we are doing."[2]

1. Weber is cited here in translation by Cascardi, *Modernity*, 16.

2. Caputo, *Truth*, 49. His account of Weber is brief and hugely

For Weber modernity was thus double-edged. And it followed that disenchantment proceeded hand-in-hand with what were still the necessary moves towards enlightenment and modernity. Sociologists have thus been engaged in reflecting on the positives and negatives of disenchantment ever since. Weber gathers together a range of phenomena in his discussion, but secularization is key, as is his attempt to hold on to the value of science ("as a vocation," no less) while still finding value in human endeavor that cannot be reduced to rational or industrial measures. As has become increasingly clear ever since Weber, when the public square is reduced to what contributes to progress (be it technological, financial, or whatever can be measured) then "our most precious values retreat into private life." But in Caputo's pithy formulation, we banish "magic" at rather great a cost: "When love loses its 'magic' the love is gone."[3]

Arguably Weber thought that science, properly harnessed, could bring about a certain re-enchantment in and of itself. But in any case, the language has subsequently taken on a life of its own, in discussions of the sacred and the secular and the search for something bigger than accounts of human mastery of the world around us. It is not my intention to divert into a full exploration of these issues, but a helpful piece by Indian scholar Jibu Matthew George traces some of the ways the language of dis-/re-/enchantment has worked in different ways, and urges that we are not best served by thinking of disenchantment as in itself modern. Rather, any object or experience can be a potential source of enchantment: what matters is the relationship brought to the object or experience by the experiencing subject. Disenchantment occurs when the world is perceived as

illuminating: *Truth*, 48–50 and *passim*.

3. Caputo, *Truth*, 49.

inert, lifeless. Enchantment finds life, and the significance is partly in the world and partly in the one finding the life.[4]

That works for me. In the right context, nature can thus be enchanting because in it one finds life. This may be (the word is well-suited) "natural": a walk on a rural trail connects the walker with life, something living. It is harder to make such a connection in an urban setting, or living entirely indoors. Clearly industrialization and over-rationalization can remove enchantment from one's daily living. Whether a new experience then of joy, beauty, truth, and so forth, counts as "enchantment" or "re-enchantment" depends as much on the individual and their personal story as the kind of experience it is. Or rather, the experience is not separable from the one doing the experiencing. Love may not be "disenchantable," but most (all?) other pleasures turn out to be. Tales of rock star excess, as a case in point, always end badly. Sex and drugs and rock and roll, pursued without reference to their life-giving proper contexts, lead relentlessly to endless disenchantment.

Comparably, then, literature (and in due course music) enchants when it connects with life, and disenchants when it is reductive, over-prescriptive, or sometimes simply descriptive, in whatever blank, dead or reductive way. But in the same way as just considered, a book can be at one and the same time enchanting to one reader, and very much dead on the page to another. Music can make one heart sing while another walks on by, unable to grasp the appeal. On these terms, re-enchantment can be understood as a revivifying—breathing life (back) into texts, music, and ultimately the world around us.

But there is more. As the language of "enchantment" wends its way into literary studies it takes on a particular

4. My summary of George, "Enchantment." See also his *Ontology*, especially chapter 9 on "Trajectories of Re-Enchantment," 95–103.

sense of *wonder*. Here is Marion Lochhead writing about George MacDonald, the great influence on C. S. Lewis. MacDonald was the author of *Phantastes* (1858), which we shall meet in the next chapter in connection with the Waterboys. At the start of her analysis of MacDonald, she observes:

> The nineteenth century saw a renaissance of wonder in books for children, as well as in poetry and religion. What the Oxford Movement did for the Church by reviving her sense of worship and mystery, what the Romantic poets and, in their own fashion, the Pre-Raphaelites did for literature and art, was done for the young by tales of enchantment.[5]

The title of her study (*Renaissance of Wonder*) captures something of the post-moralizing recovery of fantasy and wonder that allowed writers like MacDonald, and then in his wake Lewis and Tolkien, to explore enchanted realms once more. Lochhead makes the point that MacDonald's writing was deeply marked by his location in the Scottish highlands. His Celtic tradition sits easily alongside a sense of other-worldly mystery, and the name of that domain of mystery is "faerie," a word that survives in etiolated form as "fairy" with a Disney-fied reduction of the otherworldly to something small, cute, and of no real consequence.

In older times *faerie* was nothing like that. We shall defer to a later chapter a reflection on J. R. R. Tolkien's *tour de force* analysis of "fairy stories," which remains one of the best analyses of these narratives of re-enchantment for our colorless world. And that will be the time to probe the vexed question of how *faerie* does or does not relate to Christian understandings of the realm(s) of God and God's angels—a question on which Tolkien and Lewis started from rather

5. Lochhead, *Renaissance*, 1.

different views. Suffice it here to say that this entire topic of the re-enchantment of the world lies hidden from sight in a Christian theology that seeks to build itself within the modern worldview. In this sense, as Weber himself noted, Christianity can contribute to the disenchantment of the world when it seeks to offer explanations of hitherto spiritually understood phenomena, as if the "real" level of explanation subsists in a realm of scientific analysis simply dressed up as divine action. The quest for "what really happened," for example, when considering Jesus walking on the water or feeding the five thousand, can be equally reductive for sceptic and believer alike if what it is doing is effectively disenchanting the biblical narrative in pursuit of a scientific explanation *instead*.

It would be like trying to get back from the sea into the river because the river was, or felt, more controlled. Mike Scott seemed to intuit, in 1985, that that was not the way to go. On his way to *Fisherman's Blues* he stumbled rather upon a path further up, and further in, towards real re-enchantment.

I close this part of our discussion with one last exhibit: one of the twenty-first-century's most remarkable novels, Susanna Clarke's *Jonathan Strange and Mr. Norrell*.[6] There is much that is remarkable about this book, not least its genesis at the hand of an unpublished and otherwise-employed writer who rose early to write each morning before work for ten years to create the epic manuscript. The result is a remythologizing tale of how magic, which had become lost to England, was reintroduced through the largely inadvertent influence of the curmudgeonly Mr. Norrell and the enthusiastic administrations of his younger and inadvertently usurping protege, Jonathan Strange. It is arguably

6. Clarke, *Jonathan Strange*. Paginations vary so I cite by chapter only.

the best post-Tolkien introduction to *faerie* that there is.[7] That will be a claim that makes more sense, and is more relevant, once we have turned properly to *faerie* in a couple of chapters' time. But with regard to one of the book's central ways in to its subject matter, which is indeed enchantment in various ways, I would like to draw out the opening scene with a view to considering how it helps us grasp how dis-/re-/enchantment actually operates in our human and physical world.

The novel begins in 1806. Overall it narrates the rediscovery of "magic" (whatever that will turn out to be) and its reintroduction into England, set in a series of incidents from 1806–17, and thus running concurrently with the Napoleonic Wars, into which the two title characters get drawn with varying degrees of reluctance. The opening chapter, "The Library at Hurtfew," tells a charming tale of John Segundus, who presents himself to the York society of magicians under the impression that this would bring him into contact with the actual practice of magic. Instead he finds a learned society much given to attending regular meetings at which they would "read each other long, dull papers upon the history of English magic."[8] We thus encounter a scholarly gathering of experts, attending to texts by and about practitioners of the ancient arts of magic, but not themselves either able to be, or—for the most part—interested in being practitioners themselves. This mystifies John Segundus, whose whole reason for coming to York had been related to what he had hoped would be the activities of the society. But the society, with one exception, is unmoved: they see their interests as rightly historical, and it would not be "proper" for "gentlemen" to occupy

7. Alan Jacobs certainly thinks so: *Narnian*, 18.

8. This is the second sentence of the book. My summary here largely concerns chapter 1 of the novel.

themselves with "what street sorcerers pretended to do" for sordid and disreputable financial gain.

No one who has spent any time in learned theological societies can fail to be struck by this rather close-to-the-bone description. Texts that emerged in the midst of enchanting practices, of various sorts, are become inert objects of study. Clarke's whole novel grows from this opening moment of laying bare what seems an absurdity: why become so occupied with the study of what one no longer deems either practical or responsible?

The one exception, who stands out from a wider number of society members who are at least provoked to reflect on the questions put forward by John Segundus, is Mr. Honeyfoot. He becomes an accomplice and conversation partner of Segundus in pursuing the question of why magic is no longer performed. They in turn take a trip to visit a Mr. Norrell, fourteen miles outside York, who is known only for having a particularly good library of magical texts (the "library at Hurtfew" of the chapter title), but who has otherwise not joined with the York society. When Segundus and Honeyfoot visit Norrell, not only does his remarkable library enthrall them, but they receive an unexpected answer to their question when they put it to him, about no magic being actually performed any more in England. Norrell is unprepossessing in almost every way, appears to despise almost all magicians, and is therefore very much not a hero figure either here or as the novel progresses. But when asked about the absence of magic, he calmly tells them that he himself is "quite a tolerable practical magician."

In chapter 2, "The Old Starre Inn," the York society prevail upon Mr. Norrell to demonstrate this claim, and in chapter 3, "The Stones of York," Mr. Norrell does so, though in an unexpected and perhaps surprisingly low-key way, through making use of the stones of York "cathedral." Not coincidentally the novel operates throughout in a pseudo-historical tenor, presenting itself as a work of historical scholarship regarding the recovery of magic. Footnote 2 of chapter 2, for example, clarifies that "York cathedral" is also known as "York Minster," and "has borne both these names at different periods." The whole effect and intention is to paint the world of the novel as our real one: Mr. Norrell brings magic back at around the time of regency England. Allowing for novelistic provisos and license, it is a story relating this fantastical history to our more familiar and disenchanted world. (The three-part book will progress to his more charismatic companion Jonathan Strange in due course, and to a range of other magical and mystical characters before its "volume 3" is done, with the first two "volumes" being titled for Norrell and Strange.)

Ever since I first read it I have thought this opening portrait of scholarly study of a realm beyond the immediate senses was strangely and unnervingly familiar. Clarke has fun with running narrative rings around disenchantment. She even brings in re-enchantment in stages by having Norrell be basically an unsympathetic character who does not especially seek to have magic championed or celebrated anew. Rather he grudgingly accepts and practices it, but one gets the feeling that he would prefer the world to remain a quiet and predictable place. It is Strange who envisions the possibilities and indeed a certain joy in experiencing the world as re-enchanted. And then, once he has opened it up, re-enchantment takes on a momentum apparently beyond his control, in varying humorous or darkening ways.

It is worth noting that the return of magic, as Clarke narrates it, does not solve or resolve all problems. Properly understood, magic is no panacea for human difficulty. Instead it recasts such problems into a new form of human engagement, with the same range of experiences still, that remains variously life-giving or difficult and confusing. It is a regular theme of classic fairy stories that magical interventions are not short-cuts to desired outcomes, or rather they achieve some desired outcomes at the cost of other uncontrollable and inextricable consequences. The vision is more simply, and at root, of a world with more possibilities: for good or for ill.

But we get ahead of ourselves. Back to the Waterboys, and how they found these roads less traveled.

6

Church Not Made with Hands

The Waterboys' Albums

The first five or six Waterboys albums are the main focus here, since they give the surrounding context for *Fisherman's Blues*. Later albums are treated more briefly. We will stop and note in particular some of the moments illuminated by passing theological questions and insights, or some of the ways in which the songs themselves offer interesting theological suggestions.

The Waterboys (1983)

The self-titled debut album is part lyrically assured and already reaching for the stars, and part somewhat angst-filled meandering around questions of identity and relationships. Most of it has not aged well musically.[1] There is a strong eighties synthetic drum and synth sound, with the result that grand gestures seem to echo back off claustrophobic studio walls. Although a few of the songs took flight

1. Abrahams, *Strange Boat*, 50: "The years haven't been especially kind to the record . . . sounding rough and unprepared."

musically in subsequent live performance (notably the self-consciously primal "Savage Earth Heart" with its attempt to encapsulate passion in three root word-images), they are not well served here.

The two stand-out exceptions are the debut single "A Girl Called Johnny," about Patti Smith, and saved from being synthetic by a glorious Thistlethwaite sax riff; and the lengthy, swirling, romantic album-opener "December." This is blessed with one of the most startling opening verses of a debut album since Springsteen's *Greetings from Asbury Park, N.J.* began with the tripping triple rhymes of "Blinded by the Light." "December" kicks off with homage to T. S. Eliot's "cruelest month" and a precocious sense already of world-weariness ("after long years . . ."). It goes on to locate the birth of Jesus Christ the "savior baby" in this bleak midwinter moment—the Christ who in turn "we crucified." Scott summarizes this "primal truth" with "he was almost one of us." Granted this is not exactly a Christological insight, but it does reach for being a warm and inclusive sense of the human spirit across the times. There are worse ways to celebrate togetherness.

A Pagan Place (1984)

Oddly much of the material for this second album originated in the same pre-1983 solo sessions as its predecessor. It is hard to avoid the conclusion that more of the stronger material was saved for this outing. *A Pagan Place* opens with Scott's stunning, revelatory call to arms: "Church Not Made with Hands." The opening lines draw from C. S. Lewis, with reference to the end of the Narnia stories saying that "the term is over/the holidays have begun" and the departure from the "shadowlands."[2] In Lewis's text the imagery continues with "The dream is ended: this is the morning." Scott draws here on Lewis's startling notion that what most people take as reality is in fact more the "shadowlands," while the "real" world is the one accessed through entering into the presence of God (or Aslan, in the case of *The Last Battle*). In Narnia, as in life, the full and final entry is through death, i.e., death in this world, but the reality has been experienced ahead of death, in this life.

From all this Scott builds an expansive vision of all things made new in the here and now. With the full band flying gloriously behind him, the lyric looks for this holy idea of a church gathering "in the shadows, the ocean and the sand . . . everywhere and no place." So again, while this is not an ecclesiological insight, it is a terrific celebration of the sacred realm and the invitation if offers for all humanity to be brought together. The theme reappears in more pointed guise with the title track at the other end of the album, which seems to suggest that as much was lost as was gained when the unconstructed beauty of "pagan" earth was filtered through human constraint, religion included (and perhaps in particular?). It is an allusive and haunting song, straining against the sad disenchantment of the world.

Between these two musically powerful bookends some of the album explores the more familiar territory of relationships and their travails. There are a couple of other highlights. One is early concert favorite "Red Army Blues," which wails its way through a long heart-rending narrative and accompanying bleak musical landscape, telling the story of a Russian fighter in the second World War who upon return from Berlin was marched off to Siberia because of his perceived "Westernization" during the war. The song's protagonist had thought God was listening to him during

2. Lewis, *Last Battle*, ch. 16, "Farewell to Shadowlands."

the earlier, militarily successful, years, which strikes deep as Scott pours everything into the song. The appeal to the tragedy of a lost shared humanity is overwhelming. It is a hard song to listen to.

The other highlight is the thematizing poetry of "The Big Music," suitably magnificent and evocative, and almost road-to-Damascus in its intensity as it recounts how the singer, who has found this "big music," finds everything coming into color, "like jazz manna." *A Pagan Place* is an album that demands a lot of its audience: it is by turns emotionally draining and uplifting. It is also beginning to locate the spiritual space where Scott's best work would be done.

This Is the Sea (1985)

The most well-known of the early Waterboys' albums, *This Is the Sea,* arrives at its goal in the climactic title track: as we have already considered it is after looking back on his journey that Scott sings "that was the river / this is the sea." The album is imbued throughout with a majestic sense of the spirituality of sacred space, from its opening caution about not disturbing sacred ground by banging a drum—i.e., in failing to notice, gracelessly and unawares, the real nature of our locatedness—through intimations of the essential spirit of the human soul (in the fragment version of "Spirit" included here) and on to the closing title song. Even so, while musically there is elegance and eloquence aplenty, several songs along the way make no real contribution to such a theme: some are adrenalin-powered rock songs ("Medicine Bow"), while others, most notably "Old England," are more accurately characterized as bitter, with Scott pulling apart the remains of the British Empire with markedly little affection for anything that remains. This song, not unrelatedly, includes Scott's first citation of W. B. Yeats, with a couplet from "Mad as the Mist and Snow," about sighing and shuddering. The full poem was later revisited on *An Appointment with Mr. Yeats* in 2011, on which see below. Interestingly it is the only one of Yeats's "Words for Music Perhaps" (1932) that Scott set to music on that album.

The musical highlight of *This Is the Sea* is "The Whole of the Moon," an oddly self-effacing song that breaks free and soars magically. The lyric seems to be addressed to a companion who grasps the full depth of reality in distinction to the dimly perceived shadows seen by the singer. Although this is "Shadowlands" conceptuality à la C. S. Lewis again, it is expressed in a range of poetic images, drawing for example on the 1947 Lerner-Loewe musical *Brigadoon* about a mystical Scottish village only accessible or visible to the naked eye once every century. The song fairly explodes into joyful celebration as it concludes with a roll-call of wondrous images from unicorns through to blazing comets.

Less exultant, but equally immersed in the wonder of the journey, is "The Pan Within," which reimagines the same quest as inward, "under the skin," towards the true creative energy that Scott alludes to as Pan, the wild and untamed Greek god. Pan offers an irresistible image for Scott, mediated through Kenneth Graham's celebrated "Piper at the Gates of Dawn" chapter in *The Wind in the Willows*, a section of which Scott simply reads out over an ethereal backing track at the conclusion of the 2019 Waterboys' album, *Where the Action Is*. On a musical note, "The Pan Within" marks the first appearance in the Waterboys for Steve Wickham, providing a violin piece that weaves in, out, over and around the song in striking fashion. It all adds up to an impressive album that reaches for the stars, in the words of its most famous song, and just about holds on long enough to afford some spectacular views along the way.

Other Early Recordings

Scott has been a prolific writer and recorder, as *Fisherman's Blues* itself attests amply, but throughout his career the official recorded output of the Waterboys has been nowhere near the full story. As a result there has been a steady stream of additional releases rounding out the picture. A compilation of B-sides, live versions, and alternate takes appeared in 1994 as *The Secret Life of the Waterboys 81–85*. As well as showcasing better live versions of some of their early songs it includes a 1982 take of "Billy Sparks" described by Scott as a precursor of the "raggle taggle" sound of later years. Arguably for completists only, 2011 saw the release of *In a Special Place—The Piano Demos for This Is the Sea*, which does what it says in the title. The song-selection ranges more widely than *This Is the Sea*, and an in-progress version of "The Whole of the Moon" is interesting, but this is a Waterboys recording for dedicated fans only. Early twenty-first-century CD reissues of the first three albums included a wealth of additional material, notably the double-CD *This Is the Sea* in 2004. Scott phrased his liner notes to this release, on the subject of song-selection in particular, in terms of the material having "a will of its own," and himself as obeying the "instructions" he received in and through the music—language that neatly characterizes his sense of poetic inspiration as coming from outside himself, and putting him in touch with something above and beyond him. It is a key insight into how the poetic muse is at work in all his song-writing.[3]

3. Scott, "Recording Notes."

Fisherman's Blues (1988) and Its Later Expansions

To the casual listener wondering what had happened to that mid-80s band with the widescreen sound, it must have been perplexing indeed to hear the late 1988 release of *Fisherman's Blues*. One wonders how such listeners would have responded to the title track being performed on various TV shows: fiddler Steve Wickham dancing across the stage and the band struggling to convey—in the dark confines of a typical TV set—the wide open spaces of a song about escape from our darkness. Reviews were not overwhelming, hit singles were not on the whole forthcoming, and one might characterize the initial reception of the album as one of puzzlement.

Perusing the sleeve notes did not help overmuch, except to explain that the first side of the record (back in those pre-CD-format days) was recorded in 1986–87, largely in Dublin, while the second side dated from early to mid-1988 at sessions in County Galway. The green-hued cover and the motley assortment of relaxed characters lounging around in the cover photo all pointed to a group with no interest whatsoever in continuing to bid for stadium rights in the world of 1980s rock music. The most one seemed to be able to say was that this had obviously taken rather a long time to record, and had involved a journey from electric guitar and big drums to fiddle and mandolin. With Mike Scott scarcely giving interviews, what was one to make of it all?

Rumors abounded of vast amounts of recording tape, months of recording sessions, mountains of unreleased songs, and twists and turns along the way that would suggest that this one album could easily have been three or four very different projects. Unofficial bootlegs offered entire albums' worth of additional material, while those who saw the band live experienced all kinds of different versions of songs—indeed entire different musical styles—which all pointed to the wealth of creative energy that had overspilled the banks of the Waterboys' river during those years.

What was recorded in 1986–88 eventually saw the light of day in a series of releases over twenty-five years. The discussion of what these songs achieve and signify is the subject matter of this book, and in chapter 9 I discuss the musical content of the album. Here let us simply note what makes up *Fisherman's Blues* in its multiple forms.

If you bought the vinyl LP in 1988, the back cover listed five songs per side, as follows:

Side One	**Side Two**
Fisherman's Blues	And a Bang on the Ear
We Will Not Be Lovers	Has Anybody Here Seen Hank?
Strange Boat	When Will We Be Married?
World Party	When Ye Go Away
Sweet Thing	The Stolen Child

Perhaps it did this for aesthetic reasons. The parallel equal-length columns were neatly super-imposed on the grass at the bottom of the background photo of a gorgeous Irish view of gardens and mountains. It looks like a view across Galway Bay from the Connemara peninsula. The disc label for side two, and the inner sleeve credits too, included the brief instrumental "Dunford's Fancy" as track 5 and bumped "The Stolen Child" to track 6, creating an eleven-track listing. It also indicated, without including it as a separate track, that "This Land Is Your Land" by Woody Guthrie appeared somewhere on this side: in fact as a fade out bonus, albeit rewritten to commemorate Irish landmarks, as track 12. Subsequent CD editions of the album went further and included an extra song as a kind of interlude between the original two sides: "Jimmy Hickey's Waltz." Thus the ten-song back cover listing morphed into thirteen tracks . . . and that is just the beginning of the compilational oddities of this project.

As Scott would later say, by the end of 1987 he had lost control of the project and was way beyond being able to marshal all the material into one all-embracing release: "I was overwhelmed by the volume of music we made and lost my perspective."[4] The initial evidence that more was to come drifted out piecemeal. A punchier early rock version of "When Ye Go Away" surfaced as "Killing My Heart" on the 1991 *Best of the Waterboys* compilation. 1998's *Best of Mike Scott and the Waterboys* in turn included a brief and rough version of "Higher in Time." Eventually the exultant "You in the Sky" was rerecorded in a more straightforwardly pop-style for 2007's *Book of Lightning* album. But by then the original had already surfaced . . .

Too Close to Heaven (retitled in the US as *Fisherman's Blues Part 2*) came out in 2001, a full-length ten-track album that was notably more blues and gospel orientated than the 1988 album. It included some remixing and finishing touches by Scott, but even so pointed to just some of the vast scale of what had been achieved in the original Irish sessions. It also included the first evidence of full-blown gospel exultation, with the runaway joy of the opening "On My Way to Heaven," for which Scott wrote extra lyrics. But on the whole this 2001 album seemed to dwell in some of the darker places the music had been to. The opening track excepted, it was not an upbeat collection.

Some of the balance was restored by the remastered "deluxe" edition of *Fisherman's Blues* itself in 2006, which extended the original mixes in a couple of cases, and added a full CD of yet further material. Again there was blues and soulful improvisation, but this time the selections ranged more widely to include a little more of the Irish influence

4. Scott, "Fisherman's Blues."

that so characterized the original release. There were also signs of just how much the musical influence of Dylan had been in evidence (two cover versions here, with more to come), along with more gospel ("Meet Me at the Station"), and a pointer to some of the extended improvised recordings that particularly captured Scott's imagination. Thus the second CD closed with a twelve-minute mix of "Soon As I Get Home," a gospel standard that would eventually surface in a full twenty-five-minute take—"possibly my favourite ever Waterboys recording," as Scott would say.[5] The stunning 1987 version of "You in the Sky" also appeared here.[6]

Finally, in 2013 and to mark the twenty-fifth anniversary of the original release, all was revealed in the six-CD boxset *Fisherman's Box*. This is as near as one could need to being a complete aural document of the whole adventure. It contains an astonishing range of material.[7] Over one hundred songs are included, plus several fragments, improvisations, and even occasional jokes—the track-listing runs to 121 titles. There are a good half dozen full-on gospel songs, and the four or five Dylan cover versions noted earlier. The quality remains remarkably high throughout: this is not a kind of "all the takes and more" completist project, although there is some of that, but it is really much closer to being a proper six-CD album, if such a thing can be imagined. Indeed, on the accompanying tour, and in subsequent interviews, Scott has opined that this full set was the real album. The original *Fisherman's Blues* now stood revealed as more of a "sampler."

5. Scott, "Track by Track."

6. A 1986 version was later described by Scott as "the definitive one musically" (Scott, "Track by Track"), but I think the 1987 take is the exultant one to go for.

7. A deluxe box-set edition was also available that included a seventh disc of some of the original source material recorded by other artists—around sixteen songs with a strong leaning towards gospel.

Yes this was the Waterboys' fourth album, released in 1988 three years after *This Is the Sea*, and sounding very different from it. But it was also the distillation, imperfect as it inevitably was, of a true musical odyssey through a range of styles so wondrously eclectic that it resulted in an album that would endure long after the shifting fashions of 1980s popular music faded into irrelevance. So conspicuously not of its time, and so conspicuously disinterested in being fashionable, successful or commercial, *Fisherman's Blues* ends up being an album of enduring appeal. It is a tribute to a musical vision (or perhaps a set of musical visions) that pursues that most unfashionable of virtues: sincerity. It is a folk-tinged sincerity, weather-beaten but well lived in; one that longs for the touch of reality and passion. These are furthermore a reality and passion that invite us beyond our present vale of experience. These are the songs, and the invisible kingdom to which they point, that have fascinated me ever since I first heard them.

Room to Roam (1990)

In many ways a continuation of the trajectory reached at the end of *Fisherman's Blues*, and recorded back in Spiddal House in Galway, *Room to Roam* tends to divide opinion among fans, and to dismay critics. Seventeen short songs, almost all under three minutes long, take the listener on a relaxed tour of Irish folk music, as performed by what was once among the most powerful rock bands around. You could not make it up. Traces of the old fervor remain, in the energy compressed into some of the more upbeat songs ("Song from the End of the World" in particular, and the cover of the traditional "Raggle Taggle Gypsy," which is done with joyful abandon). Elsewhere it is a much more measured sound: rueful, ruminative, and incontrovertibly rural. "A

Life of Sundays" is one of the few longer songs, overlaid with a relaxed electric guitar, not to mention "electric wah wah flute"(!), and here Scott admits that "never in a life of Sundays would I have seen me here." Well indeed: this was deep into country/folk territory, to the mystification of many.

The album ends with two sharp pointers to Scott's muse(s) around this time. "Further Up, Further In" reels its merry way through five and a half minutes of a lyric drawn straight from the mythological worlds of C. S. Lewis, and then gives way to the closing title track, which is excerpted from the aforementioned George MacDonald's *Phantastes*. *Phantastes* is an elusive and allusive narrative of faerie experience—narrative is probably too strong a word for what happens, or does not happen, in it—and near the end this short poem/lyric crops up, with its simple celebration of voyaging and journeying, and "room to roam."[8] With the language only mildly updated ("thine" to "yours," for example), this is the imagery captured by Scott as pointing to roughly where he felt himself to be by this time.

The Lewis/MacDonald influence has been persistent in the Waterboys, but is nowhere clearer than it is here. It offers a helpful window in to understanding what the Waterboys' music achieves, and especially in this Irish phase of the band's history. It turned out that Scott was too restless to stick with the style and feel of *Room to Roam*, and perhaps that was inevitable. But it is a fine and fun achievement on its own terms, and as part of the band's wider and diverse body of work it remains a joy to behold.

In 2021 *Room to Roam* also received the box-set retrospective treatment, with a five-CD (and one DVD) version entitled *The Magnificent Seven*—so called after the seven-piece band who recorded and toured through 1989–90. Live tracks and alternate takes abound, and it is a joyful

8. MacDonald, *Phantastes*, ch. 22.

celebration of this period in the Waterboys' life, including quite a few more Dylan songs for good measure.

Dream Harder (1993)

Dream Harder starts with the air of a man clearing the decks, and taking a new stand for the high ground of rock music as the way to God. "The new life starts here" declaims the energizing opening track and is immediately followed by "Glastonbury Song" with its startling chorus: "I just found God . . . where He always was." It is probably a claim that true transcendence is found in immanence: a kind of panentheist God-in-all-things, "where he always was" indeed.

The cathartic opening rush of these two songs is not sustained though. As the second track fades out to a repeated lyric celebrating (if obscurely) "a green hill far away," the mood starts to drift towards a vaguer spiritual mix of traditional Christian imagery and new age aspiration. The album as a whole feels loosely rooted around Scotland's Western Isles, but taking in corn circles, Jimi Hendrix, and an underdefined sense of "Good News" (the title of the closing song). Who knows where on God's earth truth may be found, the album suggests, and kudos to Scott for looking anywhere and everywhere. But the theme of the search being more significant than the goal starts to take root here, in a way that will raise as many questions as it ever provides insights.

Onward to Universal Spirituality?

In many ways *Dream Harder* was in fact a Mike Scott solo album, and the two albums that followed were indeed put out in his own name: *Bring 'Em All In* (1995) and *Still Burning*

(1997), the former quiet and reflective, the latter louder with a full band sound. The title track of the 1995 album actually articulates Scott's recovering of insight, love and truth from wherever it may be found, reintegrated "in my heart," but its universalizing sense of welcoming all people is also clear. Come 2003's Waterboys' album *Universal Hall* this has become explicit. The title here is the name of the meeting hall at Findhorn, the north-eastern Scottish community where Scott had lived and visited on and off over many years. His description of this experience in his autobiography will resonate with any who have experienced Christian community living of various sorts, though he retains a vivid sense of how odd this looks to those shaped by wider cultural pressures.[9] The Findhorn Foundation understands itself in spiritual terms as a place of engagement with the "inner voice."[10] Its ideas overlap in haphazard ways with traditional Christian thinking. It would probably be fairer to describe it as new age in its spiritual focus, and this drift in much of Scott's writing is clear by this point, even where he is discussing "the Christ in you" or celebrating the beauty of the island of Iona, heartland of aspects of Celtic Christianity.

The peaceful focus of these recordings had already been interrupted by 2000's gritty *A Rock in a Weary Land*, an album that sounds driven by some of Scott's frustration with the wider world with which he was reengaging in London around this time. The visionary opening track, "Let It Happen," effectively pinpoints the problem, calling the "real world" of popular perception a fake, and vouching for an alternative understanding of reality, at the heart of which lies the Irish-learned mantra "whatever needs to happen—let it happen." It is a stunning song, weirdly inhabiting a self-proclaimed protected space where "grace is effected . . . over

9. Scott, *Adventures*, 233–49.

10. From its website at findhorn.org.

me," and eschewing a kind of superman-ethos for human achievement. Once again Christian language does the work of prophetic distanciation and throws a piercing light on the shadowy nature of what passes for human living much of the time. But where does Scott go with this insight? In the epic title track that comes next ("My Love Is My Rock in a Weary Land"), the overwhelming sensation is that he is retreating from that daily world, numbed and finding solace only in love—which is all well and good, and not without Christian resonance, in particular from the Psalms this time. Where it refuses to follow through though is with the vexed question of how to discern the way ahead amidst competing and fractured voices, claims and counter-claims. What is wrong, in other words, is in much clearer focus than what is right, or what to do about it.

More recent Waterboys albums have remained fascinating musically, and suggestive lyrically, but I do not find them adding to the specific ideas and themes raised by their *Fisherman's Blues* period. It is notable that a lot of the creative energy on *Modern Blues* (2015), which has a heavier and harsher sound, is spent on celebrating the escape from dogma, and the joy of the journey—especially on opener "Destinies Entwined," which seems explicitly to turn away from Christian imagery ("three crosses pierce the sky above a distant hill") and embrace love as the panacea instead. This trajectory peaks on the ten-minute-plus closing song "Long Strange Golden Road" in which there is a presumably autobiographical account of Scott's journey from station to spiritual station, culminating with "I'm just a bunch of words," most of which he concludes are "fiction." All this is (deliberately, one feels) a long way from celebrating any kind of gospel transcendence. *Out of All This Blue* (2017) opens with a wonderfully reflective exercise in self-interrogation in the soulful pop sound of "Do We Choose Who We Love?" The chorus simply asks "does anyone know?"—and the poet at least knows enough not to attempt an answer. On the whole though, the lightness of touch exhibited in such a moment has not been typical of a lot of their later music.

The exception in terms of resonance with their Irish sojourn, as already noted, is 2011's *An Appointment with Mr. Yeats*, which sets all or parts of several W. B. Yeats's poems to music. This draws in once more some of the explicit Irish influence of the *Fisherman's Blues* period, and works so well in part because Yeats's lyric rhythm lends itself relatively easily to being co-opted into a song format. Irish mythology and history is woven into a lively and seemingly reinvigorated sound, moving from several opening song/poems that celebrate the mystical, on into the bitter recounting of the *realpolitik* of Yeats's time in such powerful performances as "September 1913" and "Politics." The spiritual quest of "Before the World Was Made" resonates with particular force, with its celebrated line about "looking for the face I had before the world was made."[11] The whole album is a wonderful fusing of Yeats's restless questing with Scott's musical energy and willingness to experiment. I have often thought it stands as a coda of sorts to the *Fisherman's Blues* era.

There is a whole world of possible and actual study regarding W. B. Yeats and his own take on spiritual reality and transcendence. It can sometimes veer to an occultish passion with pretensions that, when they loom large, frankly dismay (and unnerve) me.[12] But such an investigation would certainly play its part in fleshing out what the Waterboys' Irish odyssey achieves. However this is not the place and I

11. U2 used this Yeats line in the song "Mofo" from their 1997 *Pop* album.

12. As they in fact similarly dismayed and unnerved C. S. Lewis. See Jacobs, *Narnian*, 103–4, 141–42.

am not the Yeats scholar to undertake it.[13] We will return to consider him a little further when we look at the end of the *Fisherman's Blues* album itself. Before we get there, the full-blown conceptuality of *faerie* awaits, along with the opportunity to reflect on Christian engagement with its otherworldly take on the nature of our present reality.

13. See Yeats, *Collected Poems*. I have found Hassett, *Yeats Now*, to be a good brief (and constructive) introduction.

7

Farewell to Shadowlands

On Fairy Stories

A strong contender for one of the most interesting and profound literary-critical essays ever written is J. R. R. Tolkien's "On Fairy-Stories."[1] It was delivered as a lecture at the University of St. Andrews in 1939, and published in a memorial volume to Charles Williams in 1947. A critical edition that tells the full story of its origin, development, and publication history was published in 2014, but for our purposes only two background points are helpful to note.

The first is that "On Fairy-Stories" was given in 1939 as St. Andrews's Andrew Lang lecture for that year. Lang (1844–1912) was something of a Scottish man of letters, but is probably best known today for collecting folk tales (and "fairy tales") into a series of colored volumes—twelve in all, from 1889 to 1910, and known by the colors of their covers (*The Blue Fairy Book*, *The Red Fairy Book*, and so on). This

1. Tolkien, "On Fairy-Stories." References are to the 2014 critical edition—page numbers in brackets during the discussion in this chapter.

remains in many ways the definitive English language collection of such tales.

Secondly, it is worth situating Tolkien's lecture with regard to his own work as a writer of fantasy/fairy literature. His children's tale *The Hobbit* was first published in 1937, just before the lecture. His famous trilogy *The Lord of the Rings* arrived in 1954–55. "On Fairy-Stories" is the work of someone who has just written a fairy story, or at least a fantasy tale, but is still working out how best to understand the nature, constraints, and possibilities of the form. Certain key advances in *The Lord of the Rings* are thought through in the essay, notably Tolkien's commitment to complete immersion in a consistent "sub-created" world, or "Secondary World" (52). In fact Tolkien's most thorough investigation of the world of *faerie* was not published until 1967, the last of his stories published in his lifetime: *Smith of Wootton Major*. This too exists in an illuminating annotated edition.[2] It captures something of the harshness of the ways in which *faerie* impinges upon the human realm. It is quite a sobering read—fairy stories, on Tolkien's view, confront but do not over-simplify the complexities of human living.

A third comment, as prelude to considering the essay, is to recall that Tolkien was a scholar and slow patient writer of deeply thought-through fantasy literature according to traditional and scholarly canons of the understanding of the genre. Not everyone appreciated it, of course, but Tolkien's view of his own sub-creating work in the field of myth and legend extended by posthumous publication to multiple volumes of "middle earth" lore, for example, does at least situate his writing in a particular tradition of fantasy. The world-wide success and popularity of Peter Jackson's film version of the *Lord of the Rings* trilogy (2001–3) inevitably obscures this somewhat. Deeply sympathetic as

2. Tolkien, *Smith*.

the films are to Tolkien and his achievement, they operate in a different register, with plot and plot development much more to the fore. This is all to the good for those who enjoy them, and perhaps it is inevitably what a film version will do, even if such film fans might find "On Fairy-Stories" to be a surprising and impenetrable read.

Let us then attend to the published essay version of "On Fairy-Stories," drawing out several key points about how such enchanting narratives work and intend to work. The essay starts with three road-map questions: "What are fairy-stories? What is their origin? What is the use of them?" (27). The first of these leads to the important preliminary matter of definition. The second, while interesting, and relating to the work of Andrew Lang in particular, need only briefly concern us here. The third, regarding use, ends up dividing into smaller sections on audience (which he subtitles "Children"), technique ("Fantasy"), and effect ("Recovery, Escape, Consolation"). A brief "Epilogue" picks up on the truly startling Christian reflections of the "Consolation" section regarding Christian reading and biblical texts.[3]

Tolkien begins with definition (28–38). After discussing the options he settles on "fairy-stories are not in normal English usage stories *about* fairies or elves, but stories about Fairy, that is *Faërie*, the realm or state in which fairies have their being" (32).[4] Their key issue is the way in which human protagonists are caught up in the "Perilous Realm" of *Faërie* (32), which Tolkien refuses to define on the grounds that it can only be deduced from the way the stories work. But as a place-holder he offers "Magic—but it is magic of a peculiar mood and power, at the furthest pole from the

3. This structure is admirably laid bare by editors Flieger and Anderson, "Introduction," 10–14, whose approach I have followed here.

4. Except where quoting I have adopted the spelling *faerie* throughout.

vulgar devices of the laborious, scientific, magician" (32–33). Later he pulls back from "magic" as the key marker, and prefers the resonant term "Enchantment" (64).

The second section, on origins (38–49), is mired in debates about competing theories regarding the ancient origins of fairy stories. But in a key moment Tolkien attempts to move out of the debate by focusing not on where pre-existent impetus is found, but on the readerly (human) creative act by which the visions of fantasy are made effective in the story, whether for good or ill. Pre-existent origin (whether cosmological or anthropological) is less significant, thinks Tolkien. Something new is made in the story: "in such 'fantasy,' as it is called, new form is made; Faërie begins; Man becomes a sub-creator" (42). *Sub-creation* is one of Tolkien's main insights about how such narratives work, and it plays a key role in the remainder of the essay.

The third section, on use (49–76), delves into a wide range of topics. First Tolkien acknowledges that children are indeed often the actual audience of fairy stories (49–59), but that this is incidental to the way that the stories engage their readers. They are stories that work just as well for adults too. Tolkien distinguishes between the Primary World, in which the reader physically lives, and the Secondary World, which is the product of the author being a "successful 'sub-creator'" (52). When the narrative works well, the reader enters the secondary world, and believes that "what [it] relates is 'true': it accords with the laws of that world" (52). By contrast, Coleridge's "willing suspension of disbelief" is what readers do (such as adults pretending to enjoy fairy stories) when the secondary world is not working as it might for them.

The section on children is really a prelude to briefer discussion of a range of things that Tolkien thinks fairy-stories actually achieve. Fantasy (59–66) is Tolkien's appropriated term for the way in which ("fantastic") art links the imagination with the sub-created secondary world. Fantasy is thus a sub-creative art: a natural human activity that works alongside reason, requiring truth and discernment to make sense of the ways in which it creates the secondary world. Returning to his unsatisfactory use of the word "magic" to describe how this works, Tolkien settles now for "Enchantment": "Enchantment produces a Secondary World into which both designer and spectator can enter, to the satisfaction of their senses while they are inside" (64).

Finally, to "Recovery, Escape, Consolation" (66–76), where Tolkien urges that such stories permit a recovery of the luminous nature of otherwise familiar words and things (68) and mounts a spirited defense of the necessity and value of "escape" as part of healthy human life. This includes a withering critique of industrialization and its perils, that includes the delightful line: "The notion that motor-cars are more 'alive' than, say, centaurs or dragons is curious; that they are more 'real' than, say, horses is pathetically absurd" (71). Without using the word "Enchantment" in this section, Tolkien effectively offers a wonderful vision for a re-enchantment of our world by way of challenging what counts as "real" and seeking to rescue a more profound sense of "real" that is often dismissed as "escapism" (69–75). Then at the last, in no more than three short pages, Tolkien concludes with an astonishing exploration of "consolation" that moves in short order from "the Happy Ending" (75), which of course he defends as of a piece with the "escapism" argument; through to *Eucatastrophe*, a word he coins to be the true opposite of "tragedy" (75); to joy, achieved in a tale's "sudden joyous 'turn'" (75)—"the joy of deliverance; it denies (in the face of much evidence, if you will) universal final defeat" (75); which leads directly to the "*evangelium*" ("Joy beyond the walls of the world, poignant as grief," 75), and to an "Epilogue" (77–78) where, says Tolkien, joy "merits more consideration" (77). Here joy, in "successful Fantasy," is not only a consolation but is "a sudden glimpse of the underlying reality or truth"—i.e., I think, of the primary world as reflected back from the secondary. Hence: "the 'eucatastrophe' . . . may be a far-off gleam or echo of *evangelium* in the real world" (77). By this round-about route, Tolkien has crept up on the biggest possible conclusion: "The Gospels contain a fairy-story, or a story of a larger kind which embraces all the essence of fairy-stories. . . . [T]his story has entered History and the primary world; the desire and aspiration of sub-creation has been raised to the fulfillment of Creation" (77–78). The final page draws out poetically some of the implications: the birth of Christ is the eucatastophe of human history, as the resurrection is of the incarnation, and the result is "primary truth": "God is the Lord, of angels, and of men—and of elves. Legend and History have met and fused" (78). In light of which, Fantasy is commissioned to nothing less than assisting in "the effoliation and multiple enrichment of creation" (78).[5]

Quite how a literary lecture on the art of fairy-stories ends up as an *apologia* for the Christian gospel is remarkable indeed. In the next chapter I will return to that aspect of the piece, and the impact it had, by way of personal conversation with Tolkien, on C. S. Lewis, and then in turn on fantasy literature more widely.

5. What Tolkien meant by "effoliation" is, to say the least, debatable. An earlier manuscript reads "evolution of Creation" (Tolkien, *On Fairy-Stories*, 247). Perhaps "effoliation" is the dismantling of what is wrong in creation prior to the "multiple enriching?" I leave this one for the Tolkien scholars.

Here I am interested in the way the argument works on a literary level. How does Tolkien's piece illuminate enchantment, and the ways in which a text (a story, a song. . .) can be a vehicle of (re-)enchantment? I think a couple points are worth drawing out a little more fully.

Generally speaking, what Tolkien says about fantasy narratives can be true for any work of art. *Fisherman's Blues* creates a secondary world, one I shall explore in a later chapter. It paints pictures of human life and love, longing and belonging, heartache and sadness. But in the album's turn to its gentler Irish mode of folk music and fiddle is there something of the *eucatastrophe*? Something of the discovery of joy reflected back on the listener?

Scott's explicit references to a *faerie*-like quality towards the end of recording, which I will pick up when we look at the album in more detail, suggest that much of what Tolkien says will help us directly to see what *Fisherman's Blues* achieves. The essay's language of imagination and enchantment tracks closely what the experience of listening to the album is like: *Fisherman's Blues* "produces a Secondary World into which both designer and spectator [listener] can enter, to the satisfaction of their senses while they are inside" (64). Tolkien's spirited disdain for the rise of factories and mechanization is of a piece with a Weberian disenchantment with the world. It is not that nature is straightforwardly lovely and life-giving: *faerie* mythology makes it clear that it can be just as dark and troubling as anything in the primary world. But at least the potential life-giving dimensions of immersion in the world of nature are clear.

There is also something tremendously helpful in the language of "primary" and "secondary" worlds.[6] What is

6. Typically written with capital "P"/"S" by Tolkien, though this does not seem necessary.

helpful is the reframing question of what counts as "real." Is a car more real than a dragon? It all depends on the frame of reference, though of course in the primary world—the one in which you, dear reader, are reading this book—there are fully-functional 3D cars but no fully-functional 3D dragons. (But of course, plenty of dragons in books, films . . .). So yes, readers can tell what is and is not found in primary reality. Indeed Tolkien is explicit on this point: "If men really could not distinguish between frogs and men, fairy-stories about frog kings would not have arisen" (65). This follows a discussion of Fantasy being dependent on our ability to perceive truth (which Tolkien parses as "facts or evidence," 65). The language is ever slippery, which has kept philosophers in business for centuries. I am reminded of a final exam question in my own undergraduate Philosophy degree where I was invited to (and did) write an essay in response to the question "'Sherlock Holmes lived at 221B Baker Street' and 'Sherlock Holmes did not exist.' How can both these statements be true?" And in writing such essays I acquired that philosophy degree, to prove (perhaps?) that this kind of careful linguistic analysis of what we mean by "existence" (or the "real") is worth awarding degrees for, when done to an appropriate level. One great benefit of Tolkien's essay, in my view, is its skipping past philosophical conundrum and pressing on to the actual job of talking about how stories change worlds, both secondary (the focus of close literary reading in general) and primary (the specific contribution of Tolkien's grasp of fairy-tales).

More generally, that all this world-changing work is effected in and through enchantment carries a neat double meaning. Enchanting stories leave readers "enchanted," but also serve to re-enchant the (primary) world: "fairy-stories deal largely, or (the better ones) mainly, with simple or fundamental things, untouched by Fantasy, but these simplicities are made all the more luminous by their setting" (68–69). What does *Fisherman's Blues* render more luminous? Fishermen, trains, boats, gardens wet with rain, domestic remembrances of girlfriends past, a wedding jig, an Indian summer, a bottle of whiskey, the mysteriously absent Hank . . . . Is the world more changed by the enchantment of its simplicities than by "big music" manifestos? To which the answer is probably: some of the time, at least, yes. And possibly: in more interesting ways, yes.

In a different sort of study we might return here to Susanne Clarke's *Jonathan Strange and Mr. Norrell* and explore how its portrait of *faerie* operates in some of the many enchanting ways that Tolkien describes. But I have perhaps said enough, both about Clarke's novel and Tolkien's essay, to indicate how that would work, and so I leave it to the interested reader to pursue. We will turn instead, with Tolkien in his essay's final flourish, to how all this relates to the Christian gospel.

8

The Gospel Train Is Coming

On True Myth

The best readers of Scripture implicitly grasp Tolkien's "On Fairy-Stories," I believe. Whether they *realize* that they are reading that way is more debatable, and arguably it matters relatively little whether they do or not, since what matters is the reading of Scripture more than the theorizing about it. Oddly, pointedly, wondrously, children tend to be better at this than adults. As literary theorist Terry Eagleton once observed:

> Children make the best theorists, since they have not yet been educated into accepting our routine social practices as "natural," and so insist on posing to those practices the most embarrassingly general and fundamental questions, regarding them with a wondering estrangement which we adults have long forgotten.[1]

Tolkien is fighting his learned way back to "wondering estrangement," perhaps. Lots of (most?) Bible readers rather

1. Eagleton, *Significance of Theory*, 34.

think they should demonstrate dis-enchanted maturity in their reading and thereby miss the (enchanted) wood for the trees. So I want to hold on to the claim: the best readers of Scripture implicitly grasp Tolkien's "On Fairy-Stories."

Having said that, I have read a lot of books and studies on biblical interpretation, and "On Fairy-Stories" does not get a lot of coverage. So perhaps I am being optimistic. I will call a few witnesses, of whom C. S. Lewis will end up being the most prominent, and then say something briefly about how Tolkien's final gospel-shaped reflection can help us to grasp the ways in which *Fisherman's Blues* renders the "invisible kingdom" for us. Then it will be time to listen to the album and see if it works . . . this luminous theology of re-enchantment.

There are quiet echoes of Tolkien's analysis in biblical studies once one knows where to look for them. Ellen Davis writes a beautiful, largely under-theorized, book on preaching, full of sermons that "render simplicities more luminous," as one might say, though she does not quite say it. But the book's title? *Preaching the Luminous Word*. Davis was influenced by Hans Frei, an American theologian whose work arguably pursued "wondering estrangement" with regard to the history of biblical interpretation. He drew in substantive ways upon Erich Auerbach's work on *Mimesis*, i.e., "the representation of reality," as found in the literary tradition.[2] Frei talks about how scriptural narratives function "ascriptively" (rather than "descriptively," of events and people), but at the same time they fold back into speaking of—indeed overwhelming—our world. I think a lot of what he wants to say here could make profitable use of Tolkien's conceptuality, and especially Tolkien's conclusion. Indeed Tolkien might be a lot clearer. But apart from

2. Auerbach, *Mimesis*; subtitled *The Representation of Reality in Western Literature*.

one brief reference by one of Frei's editors I have not been able to find such a discussion. That reference occurs in William Placher's introduction to a collection of Frei's essays. He writes, "Some realistic narratives, like modern novels or other worlds of fiction, narrate what J. R. R. Tolkien called a 'secondary world,' without any claim of reference to our primary world. . . . But biblical texts, although functioning as realistic narratives, claim themselves to narrate the primary world." Is that not though where Tolkien's essay, footnoted here by Placher, ended up itself?[3]

Briefer reference is made to Tolkien's piece by writers ranging more widely theologically over how literature works. Colin Duriez offers a fine account of how "secondary worlds" can work with (rather than against) the grain of biblical interpretation.[4] Drawing heavily on Tolkien's conceptuality, indeed lifting his title from it, W. H. Auden's 1967 T. S. Eliot Memorial Lectures explored the secondary worlds of a wide range of literary genres, including saga and opera. Interestingly, the book moves from careful reflection on what Tolkien's conceptuality opens up, through to a final chapter (lecture) that relates "Words and the Word"—the creative word of God in Scripture no less.[5] It remains a rather allusive discussion. Perhaps the best treatment of all, though, is Frederick Buechner's full-on conviction that the gospel can be read as fairy-tale, and indeed *must* be preached as fairy-tale. In such rendering of the biblical story light encounters darkness "once upon a time" and the king (whom the Gospels identify as Jesus) is bringing joy out of the suffering. Buechner quotes enough of Tolkien's essay to show that it is Tolkien animating his poetic portrait of powerful preaching, though oddly he too seems to

3. Placher, "Introduction," 7.

4. Duriez, "Fantasy."

5. Auden, *Secondary Worlds*; see 41–44 and 103–27 especially.

think that Tolkien leaves us with a gospel fairy-tale that *did not happen*, rather than one whose power loops back to that remarkable "Legend and History have met and fused" conclusion.[6]

Writers interpret as Tolkien's essay would have them do, but do not mention Tolkien; or they grasp Tolkien fully but do not bring the essay to bear on reading Scripture. I am sure that is a simplification, but it will serve.

C. S. Lewis may be the exception, although a complicated one. Certainly Lewis's work was of great appeal to Mike Scott, who as we have seen makes repeated use of some his key ideas and phrases. Formally, one might say, Scott works with Lewis's notion of myth enchanting our world. But substantially, he hangs back from the very point at which Lewis himself finally came to agree with Tolkien, regarding the way the Christian gospel operates in these mythical terms.

The clearest account I know of the journey that C. S. Lewis went on in this regard is the one given by Alan Jacobs in his lucid biography of Lewis. It is a complicated story, since Lewis's entry into Christian faith seemed to involve a good deal of shuttling back and forth on key questions and concerns. But the one part of it that is relevant to our present concerns I summarize here from Jacobs's telling.[7]

The question we are considering, recall, is how Tolkien's account of fairy stories relates to the Christian gospel, on which point Tolkien himself provided such a strong concluding statement in "On Fairy-Stories." Jacobs helpfully pinpoints the issue, that at first (in the 1920s, that is)

6. Buechner, *Telling the Truth*, 73–98 on "The Gospel as Fairy Tale." He quotes Tolkien on 81–82.

7. Jacobs, *Narnian*, 136–62. From here one can track various of Lewis's own letters and other writings that give the fuller, more complex picture.

"Lewis firmly insisted that myths were 'lies'—even if they were beautiful, 'breathed through silver'—but Tolkien defended them passionately as vehicles for moral and spiritual truth."[8] For Tolkien it mattered too that human beings should even have the longing for such truth. How does one explain that? Under Tolkien's prompting, Lewis came to see that myths did more than represent wish-fulfillment, but actually served as ways in which profound truths operated in the human mind, offering ways of conceiving concepts that could not be straightforwardly cashed out in factual terms, terms reducible to "what this means is . . . ."

In September 1931 Lewis spent a long evening talking with Tolkien (and with Hugo Dyson) and had some sort of epiphany. The result, as he would famously express it, was a recognition that "the story of Christ is simply a true myth: a myth working on us in the same way as the others, but with [the] tremendous difference that *it really happened*: and one must be content to accept it in the same way."[9]

It would take a while for this "conversion" of Lewis's imagination to work itself out in his writing, but it did, eventually, in at least a couple of different ways. One was the writing of many popular books defending Christianity. More interesting, for our purposes, was the other development: the writing of fantasy fiction, for children and for adults, which sought to capture something of this "true myth." In the process, Lewis writes the kind of fantasy that offers a Christian re-enchantment of the world, most famously in his series of "Narnia" novels beginning with *The Lion, the Witch, and the Wardrobe* (1950) and ending with the one from which we have already quoted a couple of times, *The Last Battle* (1956).[10]

8. Jacobs, *Narnian*, 143.

9. Lewis, in a letter quoted in Jacobs, *Narnian*, 149.

10. Among his fantasy-myth theological fiction for adults is *The*

These books do not demonstrate that Christianity is true, of course. Rather, they operate in precisely the manner in which Tolkien's "Fairy-stories" essay suggests, in its final paragraph, is the commission of all good Fantasy literature, touched as it is by the gospel: "The *Evangelium* has not abrogated legends; it has hallowed them," leading to the concluding claim that in Fantasy one might assist in the "multiple enrichment of creation."[11] The Narnia books, at their best, render luminous the primary world, though here it does get complicated, for reasons worth noting but not exploring in any depth. On the one hand Lewis sets up the Narnia stories as primary/secondary world narratives in the first place, which complicates the way in which the narrative's secondary world reflects back into the reader's primary world. And on the other hand, the way Lewis populates his secondary world, explicitly in the case of Narnia itself, pays no heed to what Tolkien thought of as one of the key requirements of fantasy myth: Lewis draws from anywhere and everywhere (famously, for example, Father Christmas turns up in Narnia), so the serious and studied consistent mythical frame, which meant so much to Tolkien, is repeatedly broken.

Lewis was writing in post-war Britain at around about the time that Christianity was losing its hold on British culture. The most perceptive of Beatles' commentators, Ian MacDonald, in his penetrating analysis of the Beatles' records in their sixties context, has suggested that the loss of a Christian consensus and compelling reasons to believe created the vacuum into which rock and roll rushed at this point in time. (My guess is that a comparable analysis could be made of Elvis, and the late 1950s, in America; or in due

---

Great Divorce, in which George MacDonald himself makes a (not very disguised) appearance.

11. Tolkien, "On Fairy-Stories," 78–79.

course the impact of the Beatles themselves in the US.) Beatles fans were part of a culture "abandoning a Christian world of postponed pleasure for a hungry secularism fed by technological conveniences," so that "The Beatles' lives and works are prototype models of post-Christian 'nowness.'"[12] In the final analysis, claims MacDonald, what the Beatles achieved was in direct historical succession from "the Death of God" percolating out into society. The church had failed—rock music took its place.[13] Whatever may be overly simplifying in such an account, it has a broad ring of truth about it. The way the Beatles captured the imagination lacked Lewis's literary flair, but with the aid of the music it nevertheless carried listeners away from the primary world.

Rock music would subsequently walk an awkward line between low-culture disdain for the arts and literary heritage (most obviously in the late 1970s punk upheavals), and an artful celebration—often in more folk-orientated expressions—of literary classics. Sometimes even on the same album: Led Zeppelin's untitled fourth album (1971) moves without missing a beat from its second song's primal "it's been a long time since we rock and rolled," ("Rock and Roll") to the *Lord of the Rings*-infused "The Battle of Evermore," which draws freely (and not for their first time) upon Tolkien imagery. They even effectively merge the two together on the album's next song, the celebrated "Stairway to Heaven."

But what I think Mike Scott discovers in the recording of *Fisherman's Blues*, and what the album itself effects as a finished product (or finished products), is a return to a much more Lewis/Tolkien immersion in the Tolkienesque sense of fairy-story mythology. Through the Irish musical traditions, and the simple act of stepping away from the big

12. MacDonald, *Revolution in the Head*, 30, 21.

13. MacDonald, *Revolution in the Head*, 6, 33.

centers of the music business such as London, Scott finds a path that leads to the invisible kingdom. He proves to be an excited and enthusiastic guide as he leads listeners on a journey from the headlong energy of the album's early songs through to the meandering folk-styled ways of its later songs. Though what he is brokering looks different to me, as a Christian listener informed by Tolkien's essay. *Fisherman's Blues* stumbles into re-enchanting the world, and how to describe that re-enchantment depends a lot on where the listener is coming from.

So *Fisherman's Blues* is not a Christian album, but it gets itself inevitably caught up on the gracious overspill of gospel joy that all good re-enchantment embodies. Hence the gospel songs (in the wider song selections of *Fisherman's Box*), the C. S. Lewis quotes that fit just so (in earlier and later Waterboys' albums), and the title track of *Room to Roam* itself, à la George MacDonald. If this be magic, yet there is gospel enchantment in it.[14]

14. I offer a version of the core argument about the links between *faerie* and the gospel, extracted from this discussion here in chs. 7 and 8, in Briggs, "Gospel and *Faerie*."

9

Song from the End of the World

Fisherman's Blues—The Album(s)

Fisherman's Blues tells of a long journey into the real world, once we know what to look for with the word "real." This chapter aims to be a companion to listening to the album. What do we hear? What world(s) are we invited into? In light of all we have thought about so far with regard to truth, enchantment, and the reality of *faerie*, is *Fisherman's Blues* a tale of being caught up in a re-enchanted vision of the world around us? Pull up a chair, preferably with a good set of headphones as a portal to another world, hit play, and let us see (or hear).

As a minor point, I am going to base this commentary on the original two-sided album. It seems likely that barely anyone would listen to it this way anymore, the revival of interest in vinyl record ownership notwithstanding. Make due allowance if you are downloading or streaming (or on CD), but the two-sided distinction nevertheless captures something about the experience of *Fisherman's Blues*.

Side 1

I hear side 1 of the album, of the original LP, as a journey. It is a journey that starts in exaltation, is plagued by flashbacks of the world left behind, but keeps returning to the journey—increasingly at peace, and eventually in the delightful presence of love, though whether of a partner, or just of the newly discovered world, is left unclear. The songs move through classical and confident key transitions, as if making up the movements of a symphony. There is unmistakably a voyage over water, and there is some kind of arrival. How the darker, rockier interludes fit is less obvious—in some ways I am not sure they are really integrated well into the finished record. But I am going to offer a way of hearing side 1 as the journey from the Waterboys' world of old to their arrival at the place from which side 2 springs, the West of Ireland. The journey from there we shall come to in good time.

"Fisherman's Blues"

A gentle strummed folk-styled opening picks up a descending fiddle intro along the way, gives way to an exultant whoop of sheer, unnerving delight, and then plunges straight into the 4/4 rhythmic enthusiasm of the title track. Those opening chords set the tone: light, cycling endlessly, and never really resolving, but soon it is the fiddle that is swooping and soaring around the melody line, typically playing a kind of prelude to the tune, and then overlaying a harmony that jumps over and under the vocals whenever they move center-stage.

"Fisherman's Blues" is a song with an unusually energetic opening that maintains its momentum throughout, kick-starting the album with one of the lightest and brightest of celebrations in all of rock music. It is as if Scott and Wickham between them have folded the air of a wide open space into the mix of a darkened studio. A snare drum echoes the guitar. The bass, especially in the first two verses, weaves its own tale: inviting us to a dance, setting our feet to slip away on the ground beneath the song. Meanwhile the vocal exudes energy, neatly foregrounded as the musical texture becomes thinner whenever Scott sings. But between the words the full flight of the music is unrestrained, and when the voice returns after the middle eight, which holds itself in line to function as a third verse, Wickham's fiddle comes back double-tracked to lead the final ascent. Hearts and minds are raised in delight. Folk becomes, or better transcends, the blues.

It is an extraordinary way to start an album: the first track, and recorded in fact on the first day of sessions, January 23, 1986, at Windmill Lane in Dublin. The *Fisherman's Box* track-listing has it placed fifth on the first day (*FBx* 1/5), right after an initial exploratory version in which the song was still so new that Scott was calling out key changes as they played (*FBx* 1/4). They got it right very fast. Still questing, they tried again in May 1987 (*FBx* 5/15)—a lighter version tending more towards the impending and folkier West of Ireland sound, incorporating whistle and uilleann pipes, but feeling a little pedestrian in comparison. The day one version is better.

Lyrically "Fisherman's Blues" is a song of escape—the journey to better days, so beloved of poets and song-writers who strain to get away from the limits of the present moment. But it is not about getting in the car and driving to Springsteen's promised land, somewhere across the state line. The first verse takes a turn straight out of left field, and opens with "I wish I was a fisherman." Only familiarity—the recognition that this is the perfect image to set the dream in motion—can render this line anything other than truly odd. We are a very long way from sex and drugs and rock and roll: longing for the quiet of the calm sea, to fish and to rejoice in the stars overhead. The one way to carry off a line like that would be to believe it 100 percent, and Scott does. In verse 2 he is a train driver, stoking the engine to barrier-braking speeds. A more familiar image this, the traveling and the leaving behind. But in both cases the singer's true love will be with him, in his arms, riding the train with him. In the final verse the two images are paired together, fisherman and train rider, and it is all about the hope of a better life—better than this, better than industrial grey.

It is also all about the joy. Tonally the opening song marches into the heart of pure joy. This has always been one of the hardest places for music to inhabit, in any age, particularly so for the blues it must be said. For folk music too, come to that, with its preference for the lost and the lonely. This is not (yet) gospel music, but it is almost a re-creation of the gospel dynamics of pop music, built from the ground up. It is overwhelmingly uplifting, at nobody's expense. The world from which Scott seeks to escape in the lyric is left to the shadow-side of the imagination: it is described in the most fleeting of terms as the "dry land" of "bitter memories." Precisely no time is spent dwelling on it, or indeed dwelling there. Rather, we are away, though singularly and unusually it is not all about the running away, and not all about the journey. Notably, it is about the finding of delight in a different place, sat quietly on the boat, at one with the open sky over our heads. The train imagery is more familiar, and does have us rushing past featureless towns that flash by, but it is couched within the overarching fisherman setting of the song, so that it seems most natural to imagine the train bearing us away to the sea, to catch our boat, to make it to the place where all shall be well, line cast, arm in arm, abandoned only to love.

"We Will Not Be Lovers"

Suddenly we turn abruptly into the discordant dark. The transition is shocking, and yet in certain ways this feels like a continuation of the previous song, but with all the light squeezed out of it. Now we are driven by what feels like anger, bitterness, and the boiling over of frustration.

"We Will Not Be Lovers" is the first recording of the March 1986 sessions with Bob Johnston as producer (*FBx* 2/1), and begins abruptly because that is how Scott kicked off the in-studio performance. (As a sign of just how far and wide the sessions were about to go, it is effectively the only recording from all of *FBx* 2–4 that made it on to the finished 1986 album.)

In part the transition from the preceding "Fisherman's Blues" is flagged by the constraining of the opening track's spacious guitar sound and the twisting of its major key signature into a vocal emphasis that pulls us constantly to the song's minor key (Am). The guitar here is buried deep, certainly never allowed to soar. The tone is carried above all by powerfully brash slapped bass notes, again underlying a steady, soldiering rhythm that never lets up throughout the seven minutes of despairing musical and emotional bleakness. Although the musicians drop back slightly for a tentatively more remorseful fourth verse, they wade right back in as soon as the lyric is done, endlessly alternating between Am and F, not even reaching to the dominant seventh (G), down and up, down and up, going nowhere, tapping into "the elemental power of the two-chord song," which Scott says elsewhere that he learned from the Velvet Underground.[1]

By the end the relentless tight harmony of the fiddle, increasingly interwoven with an organ sound that likewise does little but track the rhythm, spitting out clusters of tight notes, has successfully conveyed claustrophobia and restlessness—tossing and turning through a long dark night, in a song that never really lands anywhere at all. There is no resolution and no progression, either musically or in the narrative. We are stuck in a very bad place indeed.

Lyrically the song jumps straight in to the dissolution of a relationship, picking up the moment after something has triggered a war of words. There is momentary musical respite at the opening of the fourth and final verse, as the singer steps aside to reflect, ruefully, on a world falling apart. But, as the verse ends and the final title refrain arrives and the band kicks back in at full tilt, all of that wider context is nothing compared to this present personal disintegration, to "what we do to each other."[2]

The worst thing about heartbreak is that the world just goes on and on and never ends: as bar after bar of the galloping rhythm unfolds, unchanging, bleak, finding no way out until, right around the seven minute mark, it simply crashes bluntly into a wall and stops. A fade out might have conveyed eternal gloom, but somehow the sudden ending does a better job of suggesting complete exhaustion.

So this is the anti-love song. It does not fit. Tonally and lyrically "We Will Not Be Lovers" is a jagged insert from

1. Scott, "Recording Notes."

2. Scott would dedicate the song in concert to various disliked people, and in his autobiography mentions a complicated relationship with his then girlfriend as part of the genesis of the song (*Adventures*, 80). But the way it sounds on the record it is simply a broken love song.

another world on the finished album, unlike anything else, and standing broadly in the way of the listener's passage to the spacious places to come.

"Strange Boat"

Then as if waking up the morning after the nightmare, or more probably in the early evening of the next day after sleeping it off, "Strange Boat" ferries us gently away from the wreckage. The minor key resolves as we sail at last into A major, and the contrast is complete. There is no hint of the turmoil just survived: we are in calm waters. Musically this feels like the country stylings of the American South, handled simply with guitar and drums. Elegance all round.

The elegance was in fact achieved at length: four different versions or part-versions of the song are found on *Fisherman's Box*. There is a ballad version at *FBx* 2/16; a long version from which the final song was excerpted (*FBx* 5/14) though the longer version simply extends the musical theme by about two and a half minutes and has no additional lyrics; an uncertain layer-by-layer revision of it (*FBx* 5/20); and a final acoustic take (*FBx* 6/6), showing that the song could have appeared on side 2 of the original album.

As "Strange Boat" progresses ("builds" would be too strong a word for what unfolds here), Wickham's fiddle arrives in the second verse to add a reflective overlay, suggesting melancholy, or perhaps better the "strangeness" of the world as it passes. Although musically this is two verses/middle eight/third verse, lyrically it is four simple verses of strangeness. It is quite a litany: boat, shore, cargo, sea, wind, crew, car, star, ladder, time, goal . . . all are strange, and all are "ours." This is side 1's chief intimation of the pastoral beauty that suffuses side 2's West of Ireland odyssey.

As for the lyrics: Who are "we?" On one level it is irresistible to hear this as the band themselves, out in search of new musical homeland away from the "big music." On another level it is surely all of us, as we travel with them. The final verse closes on a poignant image for what is at stake: panning back to a bigger picture, away from the specifics of any journey that is being undertaken by the travelers in the song, we are suddenly reflecting on the world in which we live, and our own purposes within it. Here comes one of Scott's signature lyrical moves for the album. What are they doing in all their musical endeavor? They are "turning flesh and body into soul." It is a beautiful closing line, elegantly understated as the whole song is, almost indeed thrown away too casually, as if the singer can only barely give voice to the thought. The line gives rise in turn to a twisting fiddle line of yearning, overlaid by Thistlethwaite's harmonica, and playing out still gently, still strange, and still at peace. It is less the peace of fullness, more of being at peace on the journey.

"World Party"

This is the other main candidate for "odd one out." Has anyone ever thought it fits well on *Fisherman's Blues*? It is not hard to think of multiple candidates for a better option here than this jagged and angular fourth song.[3] Former Waterboy Karl Wallinger is given a co-writing credit in a song that shares a name with the band he had left to form. In a 1990 *Rolling Stone* interview, Wallinger said of the song "I guess Mike thought he could do it better."[4] The Waterboys'

3. My own selection would have been the wondrous "You in the Sky" (1987 version, *FBx* 4/10). But many of the stock-piled songs could have worked.

4. Cited in Giles, "World Party."

original drummer, Kevin Wilkinson, briefly returned for this session, hence the sound harking back somewhat to an older Waterboys style. (Earlier takes survive, showing a song in flux and still to settle, even if the core elements are all there—*FBx* 1/10; 1/11.)

But it is not altogether like the "big music" sound, even so. Rather it is stark, rhythmic, solid 4/4 time throughout, with a clipped effect that makes every instrument sound like percussion, and the actual percussion—particularly Noel Bridgeman's congas—notably prominent. It is the piano and bass that hit each chord-dominant note as it comes round, and the piano and the drums that drive the song forward. Meanwhile Wickham's fiddle embellishes wildly, in tandem with Thistlethwaite's piercing, sliding "fuzz mandolin," both weaving persistently out of key. The overall effect is that the shrill drone-whistling effect of track 2, "We Will Not Be Lovers," reappears. In the final minute of the song as originally faded comes Roddy Lorimer's trumpet, bursting through with an incongruous almost big-band feel, pulling the basic tone of the piece more squarely into the little-inhabited territory of rock music than anything else on the record. The trumpet's distinctive timbre mainly just adds to the off-kilter feel of the whole, while the bizarre and minimal appearance of the Abergavenny Male Voice Choir (according to the credits) all add up to a strange funk-oriented soup of noise and dislocation.[5]

Through it all Scott's vocal swims through the mix, with a couple of interesting features. His own vocal melody does not range anywhere near as widely as the music does, resulting in what feels like quite a constrained delivery. Also, when he hits the final chorus, with its single line about

5. The extended version included on the 2006 remaster (as per *FBx* 5/3) mainly just adds yet more dislocation, perhaps further highlighting that this song does not quite fit.

getting along to the world party of the title, a sudden burst of voices erupts with a simple (repeated) refrain of "Party! Party!" This is the first (and arguably the only) time on the record that we hear more than Mike Scott's voice in the vocal line. Does it symbolize the world party itself—the gathering of everyone else awaiting our arrival? Or is it rather the echo-chamber of the singer's troubled mind, referred to in the second verse as a madman of his own, apparently detaining the singer by running interruption? To be honest, the lyric sheds little light on any of this. If it sounds good (opinions vary), it is still an odd sound for the final album. Something special is needed to rejoin the journey for the end of side 1.

"Sweet Thing"

That something special is found in Van Morrison's "Sweet Thing," originally the third track of his 1968 *Astral Weeks* album, the second LP of his long and illustrious career. Long loved by Van Morrison fans, the song was long loved by Scott too, and unusually in this case there is a "big music" comparison take, included on the two-CD reissue of *This Is the Sea* and recorded in 1985. There it is all power and passion, seizing the "gardens wet with rain" by the scruff of the neck and boldly declaiming that the holy grail has been found. A year later, and once again on that remarkable first day of recording (*FBx* 1/14, January 23, 1986), the Waterboys' nascent new sound was vindicated in spectacular fashion by taking this run through the same song. Scott sits lighter to the whole thing, letting his vocal carry along the music, which with the addition of Wickham on fiddle in particular sounds altogether more attuned to the mystical impulses of Van Morrison's original.

At around 4:25, they veer suddenly into an extract from "Blackbird," Paul McCartney's great *White Album* ballad. Improvised on the spot, late on day one of the whole project, the whole first-and-only take is superb, winding to an elegantly inconclusive break-down that stops at 7:09. Only with the 2013 *Fisherman's Box* release did it become apparent that this was for the profound reason that the tape had run out, since they had used so much of it that day, and a further (less interesting) extract was added (*FBx* 1/15).

The effect of the song closing the first side of the album is to presage arrival. "Sweet Thing" was markedly one of the few forward-looking songs of *Astral Weeks*—indeed often thought to reflect Van Morrison's hopes for his then forthcoming marriage, although he himself was content with poetic vagueness on this score. The effect of Mike Scott looking forward to strolling his merry way through Van Morrison's pastoral idyll is to bring the journeying theme of the opening songs to a close; while the effect of the smoothly beautiful performance is to settle the soul from what restlessness has been experienced and to fade dreamily to sleep . . . perchance to dream, but definitely to arise tomorrow refreshed and ready for whatever may come. The dreamlike segue into "Blackbird" adds to that sense of drifting into a happy rest. It feels like the closing of the eyes and the slipping into the enchanted state that allows access to the *faerie* kingdom, much like the transition at the end of Act 1 of *Midsummer Night's Dream*, as we move towards the next stage of the experience.

Side 2

And so to side 2 of the original album, noted already on the original release as coming from a different time and place: Spiddal House in County Galway, early 1988. Later editions effect the transition via "Jimmy Hickey's Waltz," described by Scott as an "intermission" between the two sides.[6] The piece was titled for having been played at crew member Jimmy Hickey's wedding. It is an elegant 3/4 waltz-time delight, performed as if by a typical four-piece country dance group (mandolin, fiddle, bass, and drums, with just a little piano). Dancers were brought in to waltz during recording, to help the band keep time. Welcome to the new, feet-on-the-ground Waterboys, broadcasting from way out West, as far away from the music industry as the singer of "Fisherman's Blues" was from his bitter memories.[7] What awaits?

"And a Bang on the Ear"

First up is the gentle fade in to the lighter-than-air joyful litany that is "And a Bang on the Ear." The title, not self-explanatory to many listeners, referred to passing on a word of greeting, or a kiss of greeting, in this case to a long-departed lover. It was "code for 'say hello from me,'" said Scott.[8] Over six wryly self-effacing verses Scott celebrates a range of characters once loved, arriving at a kind of mythical summation of them all in the final verse, sung to "my woman of the hearth fire." There is even humor in the telling: "it started up in Fife / it ended up in tears," he sings at one point. It is an entirely winning performance.

The song serves as a new beginning for the album in several ways. It strikes out in to G major, setting a tonal key for much of what follows; and in reprising the clear rhythmic structure of "Fisherman's Blues" (as well as its strummed introduction to the full rhythm) it invokes a little of the

6. Scott, "Fisherman's Blues."

7. All the songs from side 2 are from 1988 and occur on *FBx* 6.

8. Scott, *Adventures*, 148.

celebratory resetting of the clock that we experienced back at the beginning of the album. The basic three-chord structure is simplicity itself, driven mainly by guitar and drums, although as the verses progress it is as if different players take turns to lead. The organ sweeps us through verse 4, then the accordion (a new instrument into the mix, courtesy of Mairtin O'Connor) picks a lighter way through verse 5, while the organ offers an alternative, high and clear path through the final verse. As that verse concludes the band drop into a kind of soulful gospel feel, organ glissandos take us away, and in a suitably relaxed manner we enjoy a sense of release and freedom. It is overall a remarkably spacious song—even more so in the extended 2006 remaster of the original album, which includes a couple of extra minutes in the fade out (as per *FBx* 6/4). This longer edit includes more of the fiddle at around the nine-minute mark, thus highlighting that the fiddle has actually been rather subdued in the original mix.

"And a Bang on the Ear" clears the way for all that follows, serving as the pivot track on the album between the journey of side 1 and the sense of having arrived in side 2. Arrival does not mean all is settled. The next two songs both have question marks in their titles, and the final two immerse themselves in the sense of it all slipping away too soon. The feeling that this half of *Fisherman's Blues* is at peace with life owes much to the seven minute celebration of side 2's opening song.

"Has Anybody Here Seen Hank?"

A tribute to Hank Williams, albeit of a dubious kind, and to a rather dubious character ("I don't care what he did with his women . . ."), reprising the waltz time of the earlier interlude, this gives off the feeling of being recorded in sun-kissed bliss. Either that or at the end of a very long night indeed. An earlier version (*FBx* 5/16) is very similar, though with a wider-ranging Americana-feel to the lyric, and overall not seeming quite as settled into its relaxed groove as the finished, West of Ireland, take manages to be.

In this song no one is going anywhere. Scott's lyric is about as far from "driven" as it is possible to be: nothing happens, and Hank is neither sighted nor found by the end of the song. There is a magnificently laid back feel about the whole thing. Musically it is kept deceptively simple. Wickham's fiddle plays low through the verses, soaring at the end as it is joined by a baritone sax that adds bass texture. Given the riches of recordings available to Scott, it says something about how he felt the *Fisherman's Blues* project had landed that this and its equally light following track both made the final cut.

"When Will We Be Married?"

Time continues to stand still as another song ponders unattained outcomes. This is again at first glance deceptive musically, sounding like simplicity itself but actually involving the bringing together of a South African folk lyric, a traditional fiddle jig (that appears in the middle of the song), and several new elements added in by Scott and Wickham. Again there were multiple attempts at this, and its earliest version is one of the first steers towards the traditional Celtic sound characteristic of what would become "side 2." It was actually tried as early as the Berkeley California sessions of December 1986 (*FBx* 3/3), and in more strident form in 1987 in Dublin (*FBx* 5/10). As with the previous song, the final selection leans maximally towards a traditional Irish feel.

It is a song not so much of lost love as losing hope: the singer addresses a woman who might be considering Jimmy or Jonny instead. In an ominous note towards the end, he makes a black bow for her "pretty head" . . . is he accepting that this is going nowhere? Does the black conjure up a hint of mourning?

Although the emphasis throughout is on Scott's vocal, it is Wickham's fiddle that really makes the piece in the version finally included on the album. Over an Irish ceilidh band playing a simple 4/4 time, he weaves in and out in more of a 6/8 rhythm. The percussive element of the song is carried by the piano more than anything else, up until the drums at the very end. For all the musical ingenuity on show the result is a song very easy to dance to in a suitably traditional style. Side 2 of the album has excelled in lightness, albeit wistful, thus far. But the end is drawing close.

"When Ye Go Away"

In my view this is one of the absolute gems of the album. In earlier recensions it foregrounds the lyric of "killing my heart" as "you" go away. Here, by contrast, "I will cry." The shift from broken-hearted accusation to broken-hearted self-confession is key. What results is a lament of breathtaking power, deeply reminiscent of Robert Browning's "Parting at Morning": "straight was a path of gold for him / and the need of a world of men for me." As "you" depart, I am left alone . . . .

This song has another set of different earlier versions revealed on *Fisherman's Box*: the grittier original version, "Killing My Heart" (*FBx* 4/16) is superb, and for a different purpose or context would have been the best choice. By *FBx* 5/6 it is modulating into a country-blues version, gentler but still capturing some of the energy of the original. The selected version from Spiddal (*FBx* 6/17) is recognizably the same song—the lyric is roughly consistent through all three versions—but the tune has now developed so far that it is effectively a new song, hence the change of title. And the fiddle solo (of which an alternative version is retained in *FBx* 6/18)[9] is the clincher: the song has become something new.

Again Scott's voice holds the foreground, but the swirling range of sound beneath it is magnificently kept in tension throughout. A slide mandolin overlays a simple rhythm on the guitar, creating a musical space that is kept in play to the very end when it resolves up to a moment of perfectly captured poise. The use of a bouzouki (a long-necked Greek mandolin) here, as elsewhere on the later songs on the album, brings with it an air of jazz-like flexibility with the scale. The drift to a Greek musical feel, not least in the slightly discordant shift to modal chords here, marks a mood that dominates the final stretch of the album. It re-conjures the sense of travel that the lyrics also point towards, while the fiddle, breaking out into a glorious reel specifically composed for the song, echoes the singer left back at home. The song thus pulls in two ways at once: looking out to where "ye" have gone away, while dwelling quietly in place with the markers of Irish music already well established by this point on the album. The listener can almost feel their heart being pulled gently in two directions.

But if the singer's muse is leaving, then in fact the place of rest and beauty that we have been enjoying is itself on the brink of dissolving. A different sort of journey is about to begin . . . .

The finished song is a work of understated beauty. The mood is kept for a moment longer as it leads in to the lively

9. Scott tells us that three fiddlers offered "reels" for inclusion, and "The River Road Reel" by Charlie Lennon was selected as fitting best, but he then includes an alternative too. Scott, "Track by Track."

and lovely one-minute-long jig from Steve Wickham, "Dunford's Fancy." The fiddle and bouzouki lead us on a merry, simple dance. Extracted from a set of three jigs, it offers a moment of breathing space between the emotional power of "When Ye Go Away" and the imminent closing track.[10]

"The Stolen Child"

Scott's Irish sojourn culminates (for now) with a song that co-opts as its lyric W. B. Yeats's poem "The Stolen Child." Yeats's vivid Irish imagination serves as the perfect foil for much of Scott's work, not just in the 1980s but on and off throughout his career.[11] Yeats also reckoned seriously on automatic writing—a sense of writing channeled from beyond, most notoriously in his 1925 self-published treatise on the subject, and also controversially as a core element of his late marriage to Georgie Hyde-Lees.[12] The Irish sense of the spirits of the land that animated much of his work inhabits precisely the territory that Scott was discovering. In his notes to one of his 1899 poems, "The Hosting of the Sidhe," Yeats writes: "The gods of ancient Ireland . . . the people of the Faery Hills, as these words are usually explained, still ride the country as of old."[13] The "words" he refers to here are various names of Irish deities. Scott would in turn set this poem to music as the lead track of *An Appointment with Mr. Yeats* in 2011 (spelling "Sidhe" as it is pronounced, hence: "The Hosting of the Shee").

10. The full set of three jigs from which "Dunford's Fancy" was extracted, "The Good Ship Sirius," is preserved as *FBx* 6/12.

11. Though oddly I have never found a link between Yeats's poem "The Fisherman" and anything the Waterboys did in Ireland.

12. See Yeats's self-published *A Vision* (1925—various editions). On his marriage, see especially Maddox, *George's Ghosts*.

13. Yeats, *Collected Poems*, 524.

"The Stolen Child" is one of Yeats's earliest poems, from his first collection in 1889.[14] Scott follows it precisely, singing Yeats's own chorus just as it is found at the end of all four verses, including the minor variations in the final occurrence. The main lyric is sung by Thomas MacEoin, a traditional Irish singer whose work had come to Scott's attention, so he brought him out to the sessions and managed to get him to sing the words in his traditional slightly declamatory style. The story Scott tells of the trouble getting the words and rhythm in sync is very entertaining.[15] It is as if, in this final session of the three years, he is having to micromanage every last detail to get the album over the finishing line. The concluding flourishes, what Scott calls "the woodland band" backing of "faery music" from around 2:35, were recorded on the very last day of all.[16]

Yeats's poem speaks movingly of a lost innocence: the child stolen away by a world "more full of weeping than you can understand." It is indeed a "faery" who leads the human child away, "hand in hand." The journey, clearly, is drawing the child out from this vale of tears, "stolen" away into the land of *faerie*, according to the old familiar "fairy tale" in which the encroaching other kingdom has its way. And here, at the end of three years of the Waterboys' great adventure, in this final musical push to the completion of the recording, the listener too is stolen away at the last. The cares of the world have been finally, fully, and fantastically left behind. Again, in true fairy-tale style, the resulting conclusion is bitter-sweet at best: peace, but at what price? Hence the overwhelming bittersweet conclusion to the album. We have arrived at the place to which all our journeying has led us, but it is not the world we thought we knew.

14. Yeats lived 1865–1939.

15. Scott, *Adventures*, 153–56.

16. June 2, 1988. Scott's descriptions are in "Track by Track."

Scott's own account of the recording of this song, and of the end of *Fisherman's Blues* as a whole, tellingly resorts to more or less the language of magic, speaking of: "the spell that descended on us that last week at Spiddal House. . . . [T]ime was slowed down. . . . The house itself seemed to have become charged with magic, and walking through its rooms and halls in the long evenings was like passing through gold light."[17] What he is describing here would have made good sense to Tolkien, for one.

Back to the song itself: musically, "The Stolen Child" continues the subtle dislocation of "When Ye Go Away." The backing is piano driven, played quite insistently with a rolling, octave-spanning, and quite jolting style, in stark distinction to the single long extended notes of the other instruments. Colin Blakey's flute in particular conjures up the drift to the world of *faerie*: the listener is being ushered away from the familiar world, and invited somewhere new. As with "When Ye Go Away," the loss is mixed with a poise and peace that brings us to a settled conclusion. We have traveled such a very long way musically from the beginning of side 1.

As if to underline that, a brief extract is included of Steve Wickham singing alternate Irish lyrics to Woody Guthrie's celebrated "This Land Is Your Land" at the very end.[18] It serves in some ways to remind the listener of that world that has been left behind, but in other ways seems to mark a brief final and joyful farewell.

***

17. Scott, *Adventures*, 156. In full disclosure to the effects of *faerie*, Scott promptly acknowledges that not everyone was affected positively (or "benignly," as he puts it).

18. The unedited version, over four minutes long, is included on *FBx* 6/13.

What started out bold, loud, structured, and rhythmic in "Fisherman's Blues" has slowly wound its way to an altogether stranger place. The journey is complete: taking us across land and sea, through dark and light, from the pent up stresses of the modern world to the released spaciousness of the re-enchanted creation. In Paul Celan's words, which once inspired a U2 song every bit as mystically charged as "The Stolen Child," the paths on which poems take us are "a kind of homecoming."[19] What the Waterboys have done, across three years, condensed in the first instance to fifty-two minutes, is to bring us "home" to a re-enchanted place and to open for us once more the invisible kingdom in which life and love await.

All that remains is to draw this journey together with the theological reflection that I have attempted to weave around it. In discursive mode, that is what I will try to undertake in the next chapter or two. In his penetrating study of the theological imagination, *Imagining God*, Garrett Green concludes his tour of the visionary potential of imaginative theological work with a well-judged inversion of Karl Marx:

> "The philosophers," Marx wrote in 1845, "have only interpreted the world, in various ways—the point, however, is to change it." . . . [But] the examples of modern science and the history of religion point to the same conclusion: that the most powerful way to change the world is precisely by interpreting it.[20]

Or in this case, to sing about it. No privatized leisure pursuit this: music to soundtrack a re-enchantment of the

19. Celan, "Meridian," 53. This was his acceptance speech on the occasion of his receiving the Georg Buchner Prize, in Darmstadt, on October 22, 1960.

20. Green, *Imagining God*, 151–52.

world. Of course, to be true to itself, it would have to be a totally non-insistent way to bring in a new kingdom.

Those with eyes to see, and ears to ear . . . let them see, hear, and enter in.

10

Invisible Kingdom (2)

Is It Possible to Be a Christian in the West?

I offer an essay on how the Christian gospel might yet intersect with the paths we have traveled, or even more, how it might illuminate them and be itself illuminated. It will proceed in three parts, via three questions.

(1) Mood Music: Locating Our "Post-Modern" World?

Douglas Coupland's era-defining novel *Generation X* opens with the story of one of its lead characters recalling a time when he was fifteen years old, lying down in a farmer's field deep in the Canadian prairies, watching the day end as he held his breath in the liminal zone between light and night. There he was, "experiencing a mood that I have never really been able to shake completely—a mood of darkness, and inevitability, and fascination."[1]

1. Coupland, *Generation X*, 3.

If postmodernism has been anything, then it has been a mood. Reading Coupland's novel is probably still one of the best ways to get inside it and understand it as more than one more label for a position that someone else might hold. Relentless, staccato short stories of displacement and alienation, all with a stunning lightness of touch, as well as eleven cartoons, nineteen bumper sticker sayings, and ninety-seven definitions of terms for our accelerated culture, not to mention the concluding postscript of precise statistics tracing the loss of hope in then-contemporary American youth. Much of it is funny in a painful way: the definition of "tele-parablizing" that captures so much of the idiom of modern moral thought: "Morals used in everyday life that derive from TV sitcom plots: 'That's just like the episode where Jan lost her glasses.'" The much-cited one-line characterization of what it means to have an identity today: "Either our lives become stories, or there's just no way to get through them."[2] Enough stories here to detain the thoughtful reader for quite a while, although since it is the imaginative power of music that we are pursuing, I shall resist such detention and turn instead to the world of pure pop.

I shall never forget my first encounter with the remarkable film *Spiceworld*, which despite its title is not a mysterious entree to the mysteries of the East, but was a much-underrated cultural icon of the late twentieth century. It provided, *inter alia*, a thoughtful analysis of contemporary existence and the narrative configuration of selfhood, but on the whole was judged to be a lightweight excuse for the British pop band the Spice Girls to sing their songs while running around London in a double-decker bus. Be that as it may, a scene early on in the film remains, to my mind, one of the most striking exemplifications of

2. Quotes from Coupland, *Generation X*, 120, 8.

what it is to be postmodern, or rather what it is to be confronted by postmodernism if one is not postmodern, and does not know how to respond.

The scene: Ginger Spice and Scary Spice are playing chess in the aforementioned bus. The conversation goes like this:

Ginger: *(Making a move on the board)* Check.

Scary: *(Looking bemused)* What do you mean "check"?

Ginger: I mean check: my bishop's got your king.

Scary: Where?

Ginger: There. You've either got to move it *(i.e., another piece)* in front or move it out the way.

Scary: *(Unimpressed)* Alright—well I'll move that fairground horse to there. *(She places her queen's knight down with evident disdain for the finer points of strategy.)* Sort that out.

Ginger: *(Rocking back in her chair and looking exasperated)* You can't do that!

Scary: Says who?

Ginger: Says Mr. Chess—it's been in the rules for thousands of years.

Scary: *(With gathering disinterest)* Well I'm going to break the rules and set this fairground horse free, and move it to all these little square fields here, like that . . . *(and so saying she moves it haphazardly across the game—creating the chessboard equivalent of chaos and mayhem as she goes—then sits back, and files her nails with attitude).*

Ginger: *(Indignant, leaning forward out of her chair, surveying the miniature wreckage)* I'm gonna slap you in a minute! *(Scary looks her in the eye and shrugs with a mock horror that communicates complete indifference. The scene ends.)*

In these fleeting thirty seconds of fun, the Spice Girls capture both the wildly beating heart of postmodernism and the barely contained rage that rises to meet it in disarray and intense frustration. Let us linger over this scene a moment.[3]

Ginger Spice is playing chess. Chess is a perfectly normal activity that is, as we reflect on what happens, a constructed activity created by its rules. The physical world offers no intrinsic guidelines on how it should be played: on the board the bishops move diagonally and the rooks move horizontally and vertically because the rules say so, and the rules are the practical agreement of all those who play. In the physical world, anyone is free to move their chess pieces wherever they wish on or off the board, but by social agreement we do not call that playing chess. Ginger captures this with the bottom line defense of her indignation: "Says Mr. Chess." There is no Mr. Chess, there is just a system of social consensus, and those "not playing by the rules" are excluded. To probe: those lacking the knowledge of how to play are disempowered. Free spirits may be welcome in the chess world, but if they want a seat at the table they will have to learn the rules.

Scary Spice represents just such a free spirit, and in a telling choice of words says she wants to "set this fairground horse free." Her terminology obviously mocks the game, refusing to buy into its world where the horse-shaped piece is

3. Dialogue from *Spiceworld: The Movie*, directed by Bob Spiers.

a "knight." "Freedom," of course, is an emotive and value-laden word. It instantly labels Ginger as the oppressor. In a non-confrontational environment, one could conceivably try to dialogue with Scary, but that would require a lateral step out of the controlling world. If Ginger and all those she represents in this narrative are not willing to take that lateral step, then there is simply the brick-wall experience of feeling that one's perfectly reasonable argument has been met with disdain. Which then rebounds on Ginger, who lowers herself to "I'm gonna slap you in a minute."

I tend to think that unless those who encounter post-modernism can feel the force of this anger, own it, and work through it to something beyond it, then postmodernism will always remain a barely understood alien territory of whimsy or downright stubbornness that has nothing better to do than give us a hard time. Scary's eyes-wide/could-care-less shrug in response is the final straw, guaranteed to evoke rage in the reasonable. In the face of this communication breakdown, what can we do?

Some years earlier a slightly less colorful but none the less semi-serious version of a similar confrontation was played out in Tom Stoppard's stage play *Jumpers*, which is probably still the most entertaining introduction to the world of analytic philosophy as it is practiced in Western academia. It is a joyful riot of deflationary wordplay with which Stoppard manages to puncture the conceits of those philosophers who think that they occupy the moral and intellectual high-ground. One highlight of this verbal fire-works display is the delightful exchange between the put upon central figure of the play, moral philosopher George Moore, and the detective inspector Bones, whose thankless task it is to try to pursue a criminal investigation into the murder of another philosopher while all around him are more concerned with gymnastics (literally, as it happens, as well as metaphorically). Moore has explained that one of his philosophical colleagues holds the view that "good and bad aren't actually *good* and *bad* in any absolute or metaphysical sense" but are "categories of our own making," and hence "telling lies is not *sinful* but simply anti-social." The dialogue continues:

Bones: And murder?

George: And murder, too, yes.

Bones: He thinks there's nothing *wrong* with killing people?

George: Well, put like that, of course. . . . But *philosophically*, he doesn't think it's actually, inherently wrong in itself, no.

Bones: *(Amazed)* What sort of philosophy is that?

George: Mainstream, I'd call it. Orthodox mainstream.

George goes on to say, as Bones turns his attention to the murder at hand, that his colleague could not be the murderer, since his colleague's view would be that killing should "be kept to a minimum. Otherwise—shambles." Which provokes the response:

Bones: Well, if that's the case, I don't see any difference whether he thinks he's obeying the Ten Commandments or the rules of tennis.

George: The difference is, the rules of tennis can be changed.[4]

And there's the rub. Postmodernism, still somewhat obscure at the time Stoppard wrote *Jumpers* in 1972, gets

4. Stoppard, *Jumpers*, 39–40.

its leverage on the grander philosophical and conceptual schemes of our age by noticing that the laws can be changed in all sorts of ways, and remarking that this must be the case too with pretty much any rule that one person wants to impose on another. The safeties and securities of modern thought start to look like fragile constructions, and for every construction a deconstruction may be offered in response.

It becomes possible to ask—and not just with chess—"why play the game that way?" The post-modern world likes to play in a range of ways, and "play" is an important concept. Is it also, I have sometimes wondered, a deliberately passive-aggressive concept?—paraded as a short cut to the moral high-ground while modeling a determined insouciance that profoundly irritates all those who think that the stuff of life is just too important for everyone to see it their own way. At which point they might typically explode, and their postmodern interlocutor will sit back in the chair, shrug, (tap their Parisian pipe thoughtfully on the ashtray, though this step is optional) and say "Well there you are—so much anger in your world. I prefer to let everyone play to the tune of their own imagination." Let a thousand flowers bloom, especially in Paris in the springtime, of course. Though the image of a thousand flowers blooming always has that shadow side—one day someone will order the tanks in and crush everyone into line. The dark side of the dream?

Literary critic and novelist David Lodge once suggested that structuralism may well have been the first significant intellectual movement to be born, to flourish and then to die all without anyone in the wider world taking the slightest interest, or even knowing what it was exactly.[5] With

5. Lodge, *Write On*, 115. More precisely he wrote of its "complete life-cycle of innovation, orthodoxy and obsolescence, without ever touching the popular consciousness."

postmodernism something comparable though even more bizarre seems possible. Postmodernism is born, whatever one may think of it, and in some parts of the world at least it flourishes, but in this case the word becomes ubiquitous and passes strangely into common usage without anyone apparently knowing what it is exactly. "How very postmodern" becomes almost a content-less phrase of vague affirmation or disdain, depending on its tone of delivery. As a negative evaluation it almost means "unreasonable"—which is not altogether unfair since partly what is at stake is what counts as "reason."

"Postmodern culture" compounds the difficulty by loading our problematic adjective on to a word ("culture") that has grown like topsy to mean everything and (therefore) nothing at all. American theologian Richard Niebuhr famously offered a typology of five ways in which Christ related to culture. We had Christ against culture, Christ above culture, Christ transforming culture, and so forth, merrily finding ways of comparing A to B as if we could somehow access them both independently and leave only the consequent task of working out how this A and B, which we understood separately, could then be related together. This model, rather oddly, sometimes appears to have swept the board among those who are concerned about the life of Christian faith in the contemporary world.[6]

But the model is parasitic on the ability to discern Christ and culture as separate realities in the first place, and that ability presupposes a certain other model of the way the world is—a model that approximates to "the modern world": a modernity of reason and objectivity. But actually

6. Niebuhr, *Christ and Culture*, 53–57. Interestingly, Niebuhr does note that his model of five types is a simplification and "no person or group ever conforms completely to a type," a caution I suspect is largely ignored by subsequent commentators.

we access Christ always from within some culture, engaging with the God of Christian faith from within the horizons of our cultural viewpoint, necessarily therefore limited but (arguably) none the less real for that. Or alternatively we may access culture through Christ, an altogether different direction of argument for which the modern age has ill-prepared us. But to ask the determinedly serious question of how Christ relates to culture, *tout court*, is to step out into a disembodied space that no flesh and blood could ever occupy. It is to aspire to the so-called "view from nowhere." In the end, much talk of culture is a smokescreen for a failure of (theological) nerve—the willingness to own a theological perspective on the culture being discussed. How much more might this be so when the culture in question is "postmodern," or at least not characterized by the canons of modernity?[7]

Here is John Milbank offering the theological point in a nutshell:

> The end of modernity, which is not yet accomplished, yet continues to arrive, means the end of a single system of truth based on universal reason, which tells us what reality is like.
>
> With this ending, there ends also the modern predicament of theology. It no longer has to measure up to accepted secular standards of scientific truth or normative rationality.[8]

He goes on from there to say what kinds of ways of living and thinking Christianity might offer once it is no longer preoccupied with being accommodated to the modern

7. For more on defining the postmodern, see Jeffrey Stout's wonderful "A Lexicon of Postmodern Philosophy," reprinted in his *Ethics after Babel*, 293–303.

8. Milbank, "Postmodern Critical Augustinianism," 265.

world. One area interestingly reorientated by this sort of observation is the practice of Christian mission.

Modern-era Christian mission had a potentially straightforward *modus operandi*: it was "us," going to "them," over there, with something we had and they needed. That something was ideally the Christian gospel, God's transformative good news that sin and death are defeated and the kingdom of God is now at hand. But at least sometimes, if not oftentimes, it was a certain understanding of the gospel, a Western understanding, frequently, and perhaps a modern one, as one might now see it, even if it was a well-intentioned project with a great desire to share a wonderful gift. It was rather like a man who had found a pearl in a field and thought it worth traveling to the ends of the earth to tell everyone about it . . . though some might say that the point of the pearl-in-the-field parable (Matt 13:44) was to sell everything one has and go back and get the pearl, rather than setting up a program for the dissemination of knowledge of and about the pearl, but then parables have always been slippery, and not very modern, customers.

Meanwhile, back home, the Western world no longer looks like an obvious candidate for its status as a "Christian land," sending out envoys of light to areas of supposed darkness. The light has faded and disenchantment has set in. The "Christendom" model has lost most of the appeal it once had. One only has to spend time in the average disenchanted Western inner-city to see this, as well as seeing that much of what it has brought in its wake is not unconnected to former dreams of status and power. Regarding this situation, the analysis offered by David Smith, in his thought-provoking book on *Mission after Christendom*, is exactly right:

> London, Berlin, even Las Vegas, are not viewed as legitimate missionary territory since they are

> located in areas that have been "evangelised." Whatever else may be said about such an approach, it is difficult to see how it connects with the real world we know from daily experience at the beginning of the twenty-first century.[9]

Mission, in other words, is no longer to be understood in geographical terms, which was how the world tended to be mapped in modernity, but in a wider-ranging and more flexible multi-dimensional framework, facing challenges not so much of "here" and "there," but—as Smith analyzes it—*secularization* wherever it may be found, *pluralization* in a world increasingly disinclined to argue over whether it matters if anyone is right, and *globalization* as it homogenizes the cultural options, reducing choices from matters of how our money is invested to questions of limited and fully privatized choice (such as, totemically, how many different ways we might order a cappuccino). These three cultural trends (secularization, pluralization, globalization) are the missiological boundaries Smith considers in the post-Christendom world. Interestingly, none of them invite the concept of a set-apart "missionary" who travels off to face the foe, since all of us, wherever we are, are clearly deeply involved in the same shifting conflicts of ideologies and powers.

With the disintegration of modernity comes the end of pluralism as classically defined: a world of competing outlooks, traditions, or claims to truth. The postmodern climate has produced very weak soil for sustaining robust disagreement. As Jonathan Wilson has put it, drawing on the work of Alasdair MacIntyre to which we shall turn below, Western culture is fragmented, not pluralistic. And thus, "We do not live in a world filled with competing

9. Smith, *Mission*, 7.

outlooks; we live in a world that has fallen apart."[10] For some the response is to return to the order of modernity and rebuild the Babel stronger and taller than before. But the better way, as we shall explore, is to recognize that the walls are down, and there is a world inviting us to explore other ways of living.

(2) Interlude: Ireland—Change Here for the Kingdom to Come?

Is it any wonder, then, that the myths and traditions of the Irish spirit, the Irish muse, and the Irish musical heritage, should appear so enchantingly attractive to a band emerging out of the stressed modern world of the London and UK music scene in the 1980s? On offer seems to be an alternative route to evading the collapsing certainties of the modern.

In an ambitious literary *tour de force*, Irish writer John Waters has argued that even U2 themselves, the most celebrated Irish (rock) band in history, are fully immersed in the mission of dismantling modern empires.[11] Waters sees in and through the work of U2 a revisionist, some would say postcolonial, alternative Irish narrative, a restless searching for an identity not determined by British history, or (though less centrally) Europe or the Catholic Church. It is essentially a work of Irish cultural criticism, using U2 as a prism for seeing the story anew.[12] He has no interest in the Waterboys, because—I suppose—they are not coming out of Ireland at all, but are heading in. The Waterboys were,

10. Wilson, *Living Faithfully*, 17.

11. Waters, *Race of Angels*.

12. His subsequent work builds in this direction and away from U2, e.g., *Was It for This?*

one might say, in Ireland, but not of Ireland.[13] When quoting Bono, with approval, Waters can sound like a writer sympathetic to Mike Scott's journey: "There's a warmth and humanity in Irish music that I don't see in the big city music of London or New York. . . . [We are at] the end of the 'cold wave' and hopefully of the hardness associated with modernism."[14] But Scott's battles are not the battles of empire as such. Though he is indeed clearly ducking out of the modernist narratives of growth and conquest, trading career ascendancy for grounded music-making—which, whatever one may say about U2, is not where Bono et al. have ended up.

In short U2 reach for the skies, and arguably at least do succeed in creating an alternative way of looking at the world. Though I wonder if it is significant that Waters wrote his book, about U2's dismantling of empire on behalf of a new Irish vision, in and around the making of their 1993 album *Zooropa*? *Zooropa* is U2's most reflective and European perspective (and by far their least kingdom-building perspective) on being citizens of a brave new and emerging world. It is hard to imagine that Waters's book would be provoked into existence by twenty-first-century U2, for instance.[15]

But where U2 reach ever onwards and upwards, the Waterboys are reaching back, down, and strangely into the invisible kingdom(s) of days gone by, in the ways we have explored in this book. Except that when one reaches that invisible kingdom, it turns out that it is still the kingdom to come too.

13. They are more or less absent, certainly in any substantive way, from McLaughlin and McLoone, *Rock and Popular Music in Ireland*.

14. Bono, quoted in Waters, *Race of Angels*, 291.

15. One incisive theological account to be provoked into existence by twenty-first-century U2 is Vagacs, *Religious Nuts, Political Fanatics*.

(3) Further Up and Further In: Old Paths to New Wisdom?

The challenge for Christian faith and theology in the modern world could be put most bluntly as follows. (Though I do note that there is merit in the bluntness—it allows the force of the problem to be felt before we consider ways of meeting the challenge, ways that will in part rely on nuancing the argument somewhat.)[16]

Let us accept that Christianity was shaped and defined in a pre-modern world, reading Scripture in pre-modern ways, formulating its doctrines and core beliefs in pre-modern ways—through credal statements most notably of all—and developing its practices in pre-modern ways. Then along comes the modern world, and the rules of the game seem to change. By "rules of the game" I mean what counts as a good argument, or a good justification for a belief, or a worthwhile or comprehensible practice, and so forth.

What is Christianity to do? By which, of course, one means: how are Christian theologians, bishops, ministers, let alone ordinary thinking believers, to respond? Is the path ahead to hold on to traditional practices and wait for the modern challenge to pass, hopeful (perhaps) that it is a temporary phase? Or is the path ahead to adapt and to restate the traditional beliefs or practices in new terms?

The first path is a path that risks a fundamental breakdown of communication between Christians and others. Christians find themselves holding to a form of belief and practice from which the rest of the world has moved on. Christians may be right (though it begins to dawn on us that what "right" means seems to have shifted ground and

16. This will be Stout's response in his *Flight from Authority*; see the next note.

be part of what the prevailing cultural debate is about), but they will probably not be understood.

The second path seems to betoken fundamental compromise. Reasons are given for Christian belief that were not in fact the ones held in the first instance by Christians who developed those beliefs. Christians on this path continue to make sense to the world around them, but by sleight of hand, it seems, since the Christian thinking being presented to the world is not traditional Christian thinking. And then as a matter of observation, if it turns out that what Christians are saying is basically a dressed-up version of what makes sense to the modern mind anyway, then why should the modern mind feel the need to carry the baggage of Christian ways of putting the points (the good, moral, upstanding points) that Christianity is making? Better simply to love one's neighbor anyway and forget about the doctrine of the Trinity, let us say.

The two paths are well represented in twentieth-century theology, as the modern world creaked under the burdens of trying to hold everything together, in a conceptual and philosophical sense. The one path was the kind of theology-against-the-culture stand-off pioneered by the great Danish thinker Soren Kierkegaard and taken to majestic and extraordinary lengths by the Swiss theologian Karl Barth. Christian theology is indeed "irrational" on this account, if "rational" is the modern yardstick by which to judge matters. For Barth, gospel logic defeated modern logic, so of course Christianity was after all rational, except that he had thereby redefined "rational" to mean God-focused, trinitarian, and so forth. The second path was more heavily populated by theologians such as Paul Tillich, Rudolf Bultmann, and the like—Christian truths re-expressed (or "demythologized" to use Bultmann's preferred term) to show that while Jesus may not actually have walked on water, the words signify something that can after all make sense to the modern mind. And many similar arguments.

Thus the two options appearing to confront the Christian mind at the gates of modernity: incomprehensibility or compromise. And if "the West" is the label we give to the modern world, the world under "enlightenment," rather than simply a geographical label, then the question becomes: is it possible to be a Christian in the West? As to whether the same problem or question arises in the subsequent move to postmodernity, we shall come to that in a moment.

The basic argument concerning the dilemma confronting Christian faith in modern times owes something to Alasdair MacIntyre's early work, in which he is in fact pressing into the "religious significance of atheism," in the late 1960s.[17] Ever since coming across this argument it has surprised me how little it appears to be taken up in theological or philosophical discourse, and how apparently invisible it is on a more popular level concerning the practices and beliefs of Christians outside the academic world of theology.

Here is the argument as I would present it—and have indeed presented it—in non-academic terms. (This paragraph recaps the above, and may be skipped by those wanting to move straight to how to respond.) Modernism is basically the label given to the period of the "enlightenment." "The West," when it is not simply a geographical label, is the home territory of modernism. The West is always asking: "how do you know?" This study of knowledge ("epistemology") is preoccupied with being certain. Doubt plays a huge role: if you cannot be certain then do you really know after all? But this particular form of epistemology, which the West holds dear, is actually one way of being

17. For MacIntyre's argument, see his "Fate of Theism." The best discussion I know of the questions raised is Stout, *Flight from Authority*, especially 97–104.

rational, one that works with (a particular kind of) logic as its framework. Now if this way of being rational sets the agenda for truth, then it becomes debatable as to whether faith is an allowable public option. Or more simply: *is it possible to be a Christian in the West?*

To those who have grown up postmodern, much of this may seem obvious. In the absence of objective rational criteria, tradition-independent and universally agreed upon, younger generations have become very used to defaulting to "this is my story" or "this is how it looks to me (and, sometimes, people like me)." The postmodern world has stumbled into the paths of something valuable, life-giving, most definitely obscured in the modern era, but all too often not quite clearly perceived after all. It has been better—to put it bluntly—at disenchantment with modernity, than it has been at re-enchantment of the world around us, or at rediscovering the original enchantment that it plainly sees had been lost.

I wonder if there are two ways ahead at this point. The first is with the philosophers and theologians (as one of whom, lest I am misunderstood, I would tend to count myself, so this point is not intended as dismissive). In a delightful twist of intellectual development, it was the same Alasdair MacIntyre who formulated the dilemma we have been considering who then offered some of the most profound ways out of it, or beyond it. His own reconnection with Catholic faith may be discerned in his great trilogy of philosophical-ethical works in the 1980s, in which he complexified the ways in which we understand rational judgments in the midst of the traditions we inhabit. In *After Virtue*, which was a seeking after virtue as much as it was an account of where the world finds itself once virtue has departed, MacIntyre reflected that traditional morality was a combination of where we are at, where we want to be, and how we might get from here to there. In other words it has an end in view, which brings in the notion that all our thinking (and indeed our living) is part of a story with a trajectory—a past and a future. In distinction from the modern project of pursuing objectivity, which as we saw ended up all too easily in fragmentation, MacIntyre's alternative is to advocate traditional conceptions (or embodiments) of rationality. But which ones? This is the topic of his follow up, *Whose Justice? Which Rationality?* Here the goal is to learn to make meaningful comparisons between different traditions. He offers a sustained argument for saying that terms like "justice" and "rationality" get their meaning(s) from the tradition in which they are constituted. The third book in the "trilogy" compares *Three Rival Versions of Moral Enquiry* and finally reveals MacIntyre's own preferred solution to the dilemma. The three versions are "encyclopedia," which is roughly the objective model; "genealogy" (which he draws from Neitzsche by locating meaning in terms of where an idea comes from); and Thomism, the tradition descended from Aquinas, in which moral enquiry is seen as a craft and carried on and nurtured within a tradition. Knowledge is acquired like goodness, through apprenticeship and a willingness to trust and believe.[18]

Before leaving this theological-philosophical path out of the woods, a couple of thought-provoking responses to MacIntyre's work that seem to both support it and point to ways in which it might be grounded in Christian faith and practice. Garrett Green nicely sets to one side any residual worry that too much ground is being given in passing up on the certainties of the modern era: "It is probably best not to spend much energy lamenting over lost Christendom, for we, like the Israelites of old, made quite a mess of things

18. See MacIntyre, *After Virtue*, *Whose Justice?*, and *Three Rival Versions*.

when we were in charge."[19] And back to Jonathan Wilson, who we considered before on the topic of fragmentation and falling apart: "the church commends the Gospel by living according to the Gospel, not by appealing to some ground outside the Gospel . . . [this is about] *living faithfully* in a fragmented world: living faithfully simply is the Christian mission in the modern world."[20] In their own ways I think that Green and Wilson are both finding language to point towards re-enchantment. It can be hard work talking about re-enchantment without availing oneself of its conceptuality more directly, but philosophers and theologians nevertheless manage to do it.

We could stay with this discussion a long time, but my real interest here is in seeing how all of this—this discussion of the possibilities and pitfalls of Christian thinking in the no-longer-modern world of the twenty-first-century—connects with the Waterboys' musical pilgrimage to the invisible kingdom that we have been considering in this book. So the second sort of response to the question of whether it is possible to be a Christian in the West is by way of music, and in particular the music of *Fisherman's Blues*. I believe it is entirely congruent with all that has been said by and after MacIntyre, here in this chapter's multi-part essay. But it certainly sounds different, and a whole lot more entertaining. This second response to the question of whether it is possible to be a Christian in the West embraces the way of (re-)enchantment, with the Irish musical magic of the Waterboys as our soundtrack. It has been the project and purpose of this whole book to describe and celebrate it, and I will give the argument one more run through in the final chapter—a word built upon the preceding words. An "epilogue," in fact.

19. Green, *Theology*, 205.

20. Wilson, *Living Faithfully*, 31–32.

11

Epilogue

The Strangest Crew That Ever Sinned

On 1990's *Room to Roam*, on its one vaguely familiar rock music-styled song "A Life of Sundays," Mike Scott confesses that he would never have imagined himself "here" (not in a life of Sundays, as it were). "Here" is perhaps folk music, or the West of Ireland, or just with that particular gathering of people—that strangest crew—in that place at that time, doing whatever they happened to be doing, which was making an album even more traditional and less "big music" flavored than *Fisherman's Blues*. In the end, "here" is the "strange shore," across the "strange sea," to which the "strange boat" was sailing in the song of that title.

"Strange Boat" is the song that both carries part of the journey of *Fisherman's Blues* while at the same time serving in itself as a commentary on the album and its making. Untroubled and serene, it pulls away from the turmoil and terrors of "We Will Not Be Lovers" and sets sail towards the strangeness, ready to be changed.

What qualifies us, or the Waterboys, or anyone, to take such a journey? The most interesting line of the song undercuts a host of wrong answers. We do not earn the right to enter re-enchantment. The invisible kingdom gives itself up more subtly, more reluctantly, than that. But it can be found by those who seek—the door will be opened to those who knock, as the king of that kingdom once put it.

Why did Mike Scott write the line about the boat "carrying the strangest crew that ever sinned"? I do not know. There were probably lots of ways it worked well, including that it is convenient that "sinned" rhymes with the "strange wind" that carries the boat forward. But truth creeps up on us often when we least expect it.

That is who they were, and that is who we are: the strangest crew that ever sinned. Humbled and open-eyed, and very much wide-open of heart too, the Waterboys sailed into the invisible kingdom. I have tried to help us, as listeners, to follow, because I think that the route that they found was one of the best and most enjoyable ways to celebrate the invisible kingdom's re-enchanting power in our own, primary, but less multi-colored world. No surprise after all, really, that come *Room to Roam*, and "Life of Sundays," Mike Scott was singing that he could never have imagined himself "here."

Room to Roam casts its spell, in the words of its second song, "from the sea at the end of the world." But it is the *second* visit to that enchanted place, not the first. It is a return to the magical land, and like all returns it is therefore part more assured and clearly pitched, but part less wondrous and fulfilling.

My own view is that *Room to Roam* is an easier album to listen to, for precisely those reasons, and that it is indeed tremendously engaging. But it is less remarkable, because the land of wonder has already been scouted out in *Fisherman's Blues*. We have seen it before and beheld its glory. To adapt the report of the promised land by those charged in the book of Numbers with scouting it out: It is a land overflowing with Guinness and good food . . . we should definitely go in![1]

Probably one could continue the "reading" of *Fisherman's Blues* that I offered in chapter 9, to take in the expanded Irish "universe" of the Waterboys that includes *Room to Roam*. If *Fisherman's Blues* is ending by summoning the listener away to the land of *faerie*, then is *Room to Roam* a set of explorations fully taking place in that world? Is its opening line—"In Search of a Rose" begins with the words "Where will I wander and wonder?"—a question to self effectively saying, with a nod back to their second album *A Pagan Place*, "Okay, so here we are in this (very different) special place, so what is there to see?" And what there is to see turns out to be by way of seventeen short songs and song fragments that are full of the lightness of a re-enchanted world. The journey intensifies slightly right towards the end, as the two final songs go "Further Up, Further In," after C. S. Lewis, and then, with the concluding title track "Room to Roam" itself, drift into George MacDonald's fantasy-land spacious place. As that song and the album draw to a close, fairground music plays, swirling and swelling to take over completely from the band, who once again fade from view, just as they did at the end of "The Stolen Child." And once again the effect is mischievously upended by a brief burst of joyful mayhem, this time not from an Irish-appropriated Woody Guthrie song but with a traditional Irish rendition of "The Kings of Kerry," sounding like a soundtrack to a good time in the pub if ever there was one. There is even a five-CD box set documenting of the sessions and the multiple takes and the live variations and so on.

Yes it could be done. And I do love *Room to Roam*. But because it is effectively more of the same, as even its most

1. Actually only some wanted definitely to go in. Others preferred the "big music," let the reader understand. I have here adapted Num 13:27 and 13:30.

ardent defenders would admit, it does not really serve to extend or deepen the picture that I have been building up—except perhaps in the sense just outlined, that it shows that this picture of the Waterboys' achievement is not merely being imposed out of nowhere. It feels like some sort of affirmation of the picture and its relevance, that it can be extended with relative ease to their next album.

What is that picture? Something like this:

We live in a disenchanted modern world. It is a little bit postmodern, granted, and there are many benefits to modernity, accepted. But on the matter of disenchantment, to borrow Tolkien's wording one more time, "the roof of Bletchley station is . . . as an artefact . . . less inspiring than the legendary dome of heaven."[2] What we might do about that is not easily tackled head-on, the claims of theologians and philosophers notwithstanding. So I have explored another, altogether more circuitous route.

Music is one of the ways in which enchantment can enter back in to our modern world. Rock music (and more recently various other musical forms too) is probably one of the main ways in which transcendence is mediated to many people amidst the disenchantment—it is a vehicle for re-enchantment on its best days.

In 1986 the Waterboys set out on the project of recording their fourth album, and it quickly took unexpected shape, through multiple twists and turns, and they ended up three years later in the West of Ireland pursuing a very different kind of re-enchantment from the one they had firmly in their sights in 1984–85 with albums like *This Is the Sea*. When *Fisherman's Blues* finally came out it revealed only a small portion of what they had been doing. Rather

2. Tolkien, "On Fairy-Stories," 71. The quote continues "The bridge to platform 4 is to me less interesting than Bifröst guarded by Heimdall with the Gjallarhorn."

like Bob Dylan recording his *Basement Tapes*, they had been cut loose to enjoy wherever the music would take them. With Dylan it took him to the "invisible republic" of old American music. With the Waterboys it took them to traditional Irish music, and engagement with the mysteries of a world coming up against *faerie* mythology amidst other kinds of life-giving re-enchantment. I call this re-enchanted space an "invisible kingdom."

Using Tolkien's analysis of how fairy-stories work, coupled with some reflections on C. S. Lewis's hard-fought insight that the Christian gospel is true myth in this Tolkienesque way, we then listened to *Fisherman's Blues* to behold how it offers a way of being caught up in the re-enchantment of the world, this invisible kingdom. The world the Waterboys take us to, as listeners, is patient of description in multiple ways. I have offered some Christian ways of thinking about it. *Fisherman's Blues*, as I tell it, helps us to take steps into God's re-enchanted creation. For which I am thankful, and perhaps, dear reader, you may be too.

For some, the philosophers and the theologians will always be the ones to offer us the way forward, the light in the gathering gloom. For others, the light bleeds through when the guitar, bass, and drums kick in; the fiddle and the pipes; the sound of song from the end of the world. For a few of us, readers of this book probably being prime candidates, it is both. We take enchantment wherever it may be found. The overspill of God's grace knows no limits, and it offers to accompany all of us, in whatever strange crew we may find ourselves.

In the words of the album's final credit, and however one hears them, whether as simple thanks, or as testimony to re-enchantment, or indeed as both:

Thank you God for life, love and music.

Bonus Track

The Album That Could Have Been

What should he have done? Asked this question over the years, Mike Scott has gradually worked his way towards suggesting what could have been released back in 1988, if a double or triple album had been permitted. In May 2020 on what was then called Twitter, he offered his "Definitive" Triple Album edition track-listing, "with the benefit of hindsight." I am doubtful such a listing will turn out to be definitive. In any case, for those with relevant online streaming facilities, one can make and remake a playlist of any length or focus should one wish: the "gospel *Fisherman's Blues*," the "Dylanesque *Fisherman's Blues*," and so on.

So for better or worse, here is my own suggestion. Track identification numbers refer, as always, to *Fisherman's Box*. Incidentally this helped me to realize after the fact that I had chosen nothing from *FBx* 3.

I am less impressed with really long songs than Scott's selection is, and I settled for what would have been, in 1988, a double album. That seems like it might have happened. A double album would have been just about imaginable. I end up thinking that they got the opening ("side 1") about right, and the closing ("side 2") almost exactly right, but that they missed out the riches in between. So I suggest moving side 2 to side 4, and the rest we get to fill in. I opt for a gospel-orientated side 3, with some of the other styles and moods gathered on side 2. But of course there is no "right" answer to the question of what should have been included. Perhaps at most this is a potential listener's guide to where to start for those seeking a way in.

What an album it would have been—running at around one hour and forty minutes. Enjoy it, or make your own. Enchantment, or possibly re-enchantment, awaits.

"Side 1" (around twenty-seven minutes)

Fisherman's Blues	(1/5, i.e., the opening track as per the 1986 album)
We Will Not Be Lovers	(2/1)
Strange Boat	(5/14, in the original 1986 edit)
You in the Sky	(4/10, the 1987 version)
Sweet Thing	(1/14)

"Side 2" (around twenty-three minutes)

Higherbound	(5/1)
Has Anybody Here Seen Hank?	(6/19)
Lonesome and a Long Way from Home	(2/14)
The Ladder	(2/6)
Killing My Heart	(4/16, the first, strongest version)
Tenderfootin'	(2/21)

"Side 3" (around twenty-three minutes)	
On My Way to Heaven	(5/17, but with the 2001 *Too Close to Heaven* edits)
Nobody 'Cept You	(4/12)
A Home in the Meadow	(5/19)
Let Me Feel Holy Again	(5/18)
Meet Me at the Station	(1/6)
Shall We Gather by the River	(4/19)

"Side 4" (around twenty-seven minutes)	
Carolan's Welcome	(6/16)
And a Bang on the Ear	(6/4, in the original 1986 edit)
When Will We Be Married	(6/10)
When Ye Go Away	(6/17)
Dunford's Fancy	(6/21)
The Stolen Child	(6/22)
This Land Is Your Land	(6/13, in the original 1986 fragment edit)

Bibliography

(1) The Waterboys' Albums

Only original studio albums are listed here:

The Waterboys. Chrysalis, 1983. Extended version 2002.
A Pagan Place. Ensign, 1984. Extended version 2002.
This Is the Sea. Ensign, 1985. 2CD version 2004.
Fisherman's Blues. Ensign, 1988. 2CD version 2006.
Room to Roam. Ensign, 1990. 2CD version 2008.
Dream Harder. Geffen, 1993.
Bring 'Em All In. Chrysalis, 1995. Released as "Mike Scott."
Still Burning. Chrysalis, 1997. Released as "Mike Scott."
A Rock in the Weary Land. RCA, 2000.
Universal Hall. Puck, 2003.
Book of Lightning. W14/Universal, 2007.
An Appointment with Mr. Yeats. Proper, 2011.
Modern Blues. Harlequin and Clown, 2015.
Out of All This Blue. BMG, 2017.
Where the Action Is. Cooking Vinyl, 2019.
Good Luck, Seeker. Cooking Vinyl, 2020.
All Souls Hill. Cooking Vinyl, 2022.

(2) Other References

Abrahams, Ian. *Strange Boat: Mike Scott and the Waterboys*. London: SAF, 2007.

Auden, W. H. *Secondary Worlds*. London: Faber & Faber, 1968.

Auerbach, Erich. *Mimesis: The Representation of Reality in Western Literature*. Princeton: Princeton University Press, 1953.

Briggs, Richard S. "The Gospel and *Faerie*: On Tolkien and the Re-enchantment of Narrative." *Glass* 37 (2024) 30–38.

———. "Sarajevo and the PopMart Lemon: The Fractured Form and Function of U2's Walk through the Valley of the Shadow of Death." In *U2 and the Religious Impulse: Take Me Higher*, edited by Scott Calhoun, 75–86 and 209. London: Bloomsbury Academic, 2018.

Buechner, Frederick. *Telling the Truth: The Gospel as Tragedy, Comedy and Fairy Tale*. New York: Harper and Row, 1977.

Caputo, John D. *Truth: The Search for Wisdom in a Postmodern Age*. London: Penguin, 2013.

Cascardi, Anthony J. *The Subject of Modernity*. Literature, Culture, Theory 3. Cambridge: Cambridge University Press, 1992.

Celan, Paul. "The Meridian." In *Collected Prose*, translated by Rosemary Waldrop, 37–55. New York: Routledge, 2003.

Clarke, Susanna. *Jonathan Strange and Mr. Norrell*. London: Bloomsbury, 2004.

Coupland, Douglas. *Generation X: Tales from an Accelerated Culture*. London: Abacus, 1992.

Davis, Ellen F. *Preaching the Luminous Word: Biblical Sermons and Homiletical Essays*. With Austin McIver Dennis. Grand Rapids: Eerdmans, 2016.

Duriez, Colin. "The Theology of Fantasy in Lewis and Tolkien." *Themelios* 23 (1998) 35–51.

Eagleton, Terry. *The Significance of Theory*. Bucknell Lectures in Literary Theory. Oxford: Blackwell, 1990.

Eno, Brian. "Free, Open Spaces: Brian Eno's Favourite Records." https://thequietus.com/articles/20034-brian-eno-favourite-records-interview?page=2.

Flieger, Verlyn, and Douglas A. Anderson. "Introduction." In *Tolkien on Fairy-stories: Expanded Edition, with Commentary and Notes*, edited by Verlyn Flieger and Douglas A. Anderson, 9–23. London: HarperCollins, 2014.

George, Jibu Matthew. "Exploring the Changing Contours of 'Enchantment.'" *Implicit Religion* 24 (2021) 111–28.

———. *The Ontology of Gods: An Account of Enchantment, Disenchantment, and Re-enchantment.* London: Palgrave Macmillan, 2017.

Giles, Jeff. "World Party: Pure Pop for Party People." *Rolling Stone*, June 28, 1990. https://www.rollingstone.com/music/music-news/world-party-pure-pop-for-party-people-234806/.

Green, Garrett. *Imagining God: Theology and the Religious Imagination.* Grand Rapids: Eerdmans, 1989.

———. *Theology, Hermeneutics, and Imagination: The Crisis of Interpretation at the End of Modernity.* Cambridge: Cambridge University Press, 2000.

Griffin, Sid. *Million Dollar Bash: Bob Dylan, the Band, and the Basement Tapes.* London: Jawbone, 2014.

Hassett, Joseph M. *Yeats Now: Echoing into Life.* Dublin: Lilliput, 2020.

Jacobs, Alan. "The Chronicles of Narnia." In *The Cambridge Companion to C. S. Lewis*, edited by Robert MacSwain and Michael Ward, 265–80. Cambridge: Cambridge University Press, 2010.

———. "The Far Invisible: Thomas Pynchon as America's Theologian." *The Hedgehog Review: Critical Reflections on Contemporary Culture* 25 (2023).

———. *The Narnian: The Life and Imagination of C. S. Lewis.* London: SPCK, 2005.

Kant, Immanuel. "An Answer to the Question, 'What Is Enlightenment?'" In *Practical Philosophy*, edited by Mary J. Gregor, 11–22. Cambridge: Cambridge University Press, 1999.

Lewis, C. S. *The Great Divorce: A Dream.* London: Centenary, 1946.

———. *The Last Battle.* London: Head, 1956.

———. *The Lion, the Witch, and the Wardrobe.* London: Head, 1950.

———. "Meditation in a Toolshed." In *First and Second Things*, 40–44. London: Fount, 1985.

———. *The Oxford History of English Literature.* Vol. 3, *English Literature in the Sixteenth Century Excluding Drama.* Oxford: Oxford University Press, 1954.

Lochhead, Marion. *The Renaissance of Wonder in Children's Literature.* Edinburgh: Canongate, 1977.

Lodge, David. *Write On: Occasional Essays, 1965–1985.* London: Penguin, 1986.

MacDonald, George. *Phantastes: A Faerie Romance.* Grand Rapids: Eerdmans, 1981.

MacDonald, Ian. *Revolution in the Head: The Beatles' Records and the Sixties.* 2nd rev. ed. London: Pimlico, 2005.

MacIntyre, Alasdair. *After Virtue: A Study in Moral Theory*. Notre Dame: University of Notre Dame Press, 1981.

———. "The Fate of Theism." In *The Religious Significance of Atheism*, by Alasdair MacIntyre and Paul Ricoeur, 3–29. New York: Columbia University Press, 1968.

———. *Three Rival Versions of Moral Enquiry: Encyclopaedia, Genealogy, and Tradition*. The Gifford Lectures. Notre Dame: University of Notre Dame Press, 1990.

———. *Whose Justice? Which Rationality?* Notre Dame: University of Notre Dame Press, 1988.

Maddox, Brenda. *George's Ghosts: A New Life of W. B. Yeats*. London: Picador, 2000.

Marcus, Greil. *Invisible Republic: Bob Dylan's Basement Tapes*. London: Picador, 1997.

McLaughlin, Noel, and Martin McLoone. *Rock and Popular Music in Ireland: Before and After U2*. Dublin: Irish Academics Press, 2012.

Milbank, John. "Postmodern Critical Augustinianism: A Short *Summa* in Forty-Two Responses to Unasked Questions." In *The Postmodern God: A Theological Reader*, edited by Graham Ward, 265–78. Oxford: Blackwell, 1997.

Niebuhr, Richard. *Christ and Culture*. London: Faber and Faber, 1952.

O'Connor, Nuala. "Ireland." In *World Music: The Rough Guide: Africa, Europe, and the Middle East: An A-Z of the Music, Musicians, and Discs*, edited by Simon Broughton et al., 170–88. London: Rough Guides, 1999.

Placher, William C. "Introduction." In *Theology and Narrative: Selected Essays*, edited by George Hunsinger and William C. Placher, 3–25. Oxford: Oxford University Press, 1993.

Scott, Mike. *Adventures of a Waterboy*. London: Jawbone, 2012.

———. "The Day I Downloaded Myself." *The Guardian*, March 23, 2007. https://www.theguardian.com/music/2007/mar/23/popandrock2.

———. "Fisherman's Blues, Roots, and the Celtic Soul." Liner notes. 2006 2-CD edition of *Fisherman's Blues*.

———. "Recording Notes." Liner notes. 2004 2-CD edition of *This Is The Sea*.

———. "Track by Track." Liner notes to 2013 6-CD *Fisherman's Box*.

Searle, Alison. *"The Eyes of Your Heart": Literary and Theological Trajectories of Imagining Biblically*. Paternoster Theological Monographs. Eugene, OR: Wipf & Stock, 2008.

Smith, David. *Mission after Christendom*. London: Darton, Longman, and Todd, 2003.

Spiers, Bob, dir. *Spiceworld: The Movie*. Polygram Filmed Entertainment, 1997.

Stoppard, Tom. *Jumpers*. London: Faber and Faber, 1986.

Stout, Jeffrey. *Ethics after Babel*. 2nd ed. Princeton: Princeton University Press, 2001.

———. *The Flight from Authority: Religion, Morality, and the Quest for Autonomy*. Notre Dame: University of Notre Dame Press, 1981.

Tolkien, J. R. R. "On Fairy-Stories." In *Tolkien on Fairy-Stories: Expanded Edition, with Commentary and Notes*, edited by Verlyn Flieger and Douglas A. Anderson, 27–84. London: HarperCollins, 2014.

———. *Smith of Wootton Major*. Edited by Verlyn Flieger. London: HarperCollins, 2005.

Vagacs, Robert. *Religious Nuts, Political Fanatics: U2 in Theological Perspective*. Eugene, OR: Cascade, 2005.

Waters, John. *Race of Angels: Ireland and the Genesis of U2*. Belfast: Blackstaff, 1994.

———. *Was It for This? Why Ireland Lost the Plot*. Dublin: Transworld Ireland, 2012.

Wilson, Jonathan R. *Living Faithfully in a Fragmented World: From* After Virtue *to a New Monasticism*. 2nd ed. Eugene, OR: Cascade, 2010.

Yeats, W. B. *Collected Poems*. London: Picador, 1990.

Index

Name Index

The Waterboys, their members, and those directly involved in their recordings, are not noted.

Scripture Index

www.ingramcontent.com/pod-product-compliance
Lightning Source LLC
LaVergne TN
LVHW051005080826
845145LV00009B/2464

* 9 7 8 1 5 3 2 6 0 7 8 2 0 *